SERVICE BOOK

The United Reformed Church
in the United Kingdom

OXFORD UNIVERSITY PRESS
1989

Oxford University Press, Walton Street, Oxford OX2 6DP
Oxford New York Toronto
Delhi Bombay Calcutta Madras Karachi
Petaling Jaya Singapore Hong Kong Tokyo
Nairobi Dar es Salaam Cape Town
Melbourne Auckland
and associated companies in
Berlin Ibadan

Oxford is a trade mark of Oxford University Press

© *The United Reformed Church 1989*

Reprinted in 1990

All rights reserved. No part of this publication may be reproduced, stored in a retrieval system, or transmitted, in any form or by any means, electronic, mechanical, photocopying, recording, or otherwise, without the prior permission of Oxford University Press

ISBN 0-19-146902 5

Printed in Great Britain

CONTENTS

Preface	vi
General Notes	ix
Order of Worship	1
Second Order of Worship	23
Baptism Service	31
Thanksgiving for the Birth of a Child	37
Confirmation Service	41
Renewal of Baptismal Promises	45
Reception of Members from Other Churches	47
Wedding Service	49
Blessing of a Civil Marriage	61
The Funeral	67
Ordination and Induction of Ministers	85
Commissioning of Church-Related Community Workers	93
Ordination and Induction of Elders	97
Commissioning of Accredited Lay Preachers	101
Service for Healing	105
The Lord's Prayer	111
Creeds	113
Confession of Faith	115
Statement concerning the Nature, Faith, and Order of the United Reformed Church	117
Calendar and Lectionary	121
Acknowledgements	131

PREFACE

IN 1985, the General Assembly of the United Reformed Church decided that *A Book of Services*, published in 1980 was in need of revision. The work of revision was committed to the Doctrine and Worship Committee. The demand for revision after so short a time was due to changes both in our apprehension of what is appropriate language for worship—particularly in the matter of inclusive language—and in the constitution of the URC, to whose numbers were added in 1981 members of the Reformed Association of Churches of Christ in Great Britain and Ireland. To such considerations can be added the influence of cross-fertilization between the separated Christian traditions as they increasingly join in worship, action, and study.

Together, such factors explain the otherwise surprisingly frequent publication of such books by a church whose history is in part shaped by the rejection of legally imposed Prayer Books. The Reformed tradition continues to reject as a denial of the nature of Christian worship the imposition of fixed forms of service. Yet its forms do for the most part follow a common general pattern and, indeed, in many respects reflect something of a convergence with other traditions.

The URC shares with other churches the conviction that worship is the centre of all that the Church is and does. That worship takes its reality from the presence of the risen Christ in the congregation; through him the Holy Spirit lifts the people up to God the Father, creator, ruler, and redeemer of all things. Thus it is that 'The worship of the local church is an expression of the worship of the whole people of God' (*Basis of Union*, 25). In response to the presence of Christ, made known by the Spirit especially in Scripture and the preaching of the Word, the Church gives praise to God by offering its life and the life of the world in prayer, hymn, and sacrament.

This *Service Book* is a resource book for all those who lead worship, and not an official manual; and yet it follows customs and precedents long since established. Christian worship began with the ordering around the gospel about Jesus of forms taken from Jewish worship. The Lord's Supper derives not only from the Upper Room, but from Old Testament traditions of sacrifice, particularly those of Passover and Day of Atonement. They, in their turn, derive from Israel's apprehension of God's love in creation and his great historic acts of salvation, fulfilled as they are in Christ. Similarly baptism, the rite of initiation into the body of Christ, derives from the saving death of Christ, but at the same time takes its shape both from Jewish rites of initiation and from John the Baptist's baptism of repentance, undergone by Jesus as part of his identification with our fallen humanity.

The forms of worship offered in this book reach back through Christian history both to those biblical beginnings and to their development in the early centuries of the Church's life. But it is to the Reformation, and perhaps especially to John Calvin, that they owe their particular shape. For Calvin, the Church was to be found wherever the Word was truly preached and the sacraments of Baptism and the Lord's Supper were duly administered, and this book maintains that two-fold emphasis. One of its ancestors is the *Westminster Directory*, approved by the Commonwealth Parliament in 1645. Revealing influences from Geneva, Scotland, and the Netherlands, it listed the necessary components of worship, gave instructions on prayer and preaching, but also allowed flexibility and encouraged free prayer. Influences on this present book are not only that tradition, but more recent developments within and without the URC, as will be apparent from the page of acknowledgements.

The contents of the book reveal some variations from its predecessor. Omitted are orders for which there is less frequent call, for example, those concerned with the laying of foundation stones or dedication of church property. Such orders will be made available in another way. The additions, too, mark the changed times, or awareness of changes, that have made themselves felt since the previous publication. One is an order for the renewal of baptismal promises which will, we hope, help to deepen the seriousness with which the sacrament is regarded and provide a resource for the pastoral care of those who feel the need for some public reaffirmation of their membership of the body of Christ.

Another innovation is the production of a second order of worship, which is designed to reflect the traditions particularly of those who were formerly members of the Churches of Christ.

At the head of the book come those two central forms, Baptism and the Lord's Supper, of which something has already been said. Alongside them are other forms which are required for living together as a community of worship, particularly for the celebration and inauguration of new steps in the life of the church or its members, such as the ordination or induction of ministers, marriages and funerals. The continuing reappropriation in many churches of the ministry of healing has led, following the precedent of the previous book, to the publication of an order for healing. For this, most of the work has been done by members of the Health and Healing Committee. I am grateful also to Mary Frost and Charles Brock for much of the work on which I have drawn in composing this Preface.

In the name of the Committee.

Colin Gunton
Convener
March 1989

CONTRIBUTORS

J C Brock; D P Thompson; K C Fabricius; C A McIlhagga; J S Wyatt; C P Thompson; M H Cressey; J H Taylor; S Durber.

GENERAL NOTES

Freedom In Worship

Material in this book is based on historic and contemporary Reformed services, enriched with contributions from other traditions. It is not intended to constrain our treasured tradition of freedom in worship, but to help leaders with models in which local variety can be incorporated. Churches are free to develop their own forms but the Reformed tradition worldwide is aware of a movement towards greater unity in worship.

Congregational Participation

Responses and other words for congregations to say are printed in bold type whilst the leader's words are in ordinary type. References in brackets at the head of items are to those which may be found for congregational use in the companion hymn book.

Posture and Movement

Churches vary in their customs over standing, sitting, and other movements, and therefore no directions are given about these matters. Rubrics have been minimized. Those responsible for services will need to give clear directions to their congregations.

Hymns

Because churches differ in their use of hymns, and services too may vary from time to time, the placing of hymns has not been included and will need to be inserted by those leading. This rule does not apply to weddings and funerals.

Other Services

Services of an occasional and special kind, such as for commissioning missionaries, induction of Provincial Moderators, stone-laying or dedicating property, may be obtained from Provincial Synod Offices or Church House.

The service for the Commissioning of Church-Related Community Workers has been included at special request since it has not previously been published.

ORDER OF WORSHIP

1. Scripture Sentences
2. Prayer of Approach
3. Confession of Sin
4. Assurance of Pardon
5. Kyries
6. Gloria in Excelsis
7. Prayer for Grace or Collect

THE MINISTRY OF THE WORD

8. Theme Introduction
9. Old Testament Reading (and/or New Testament Reading)
10. Psalm, Canticle, or Anthem
11. New Testament Reading (or Readings: Epistle and Gospel)
12. Sermon
13. Creed; Confession of Faith, or Prayer
14. Notices
15. Special Acts
16. Intercession

THE SACRAMENT OF THE LORD'S SUPPER

17. Invitation
18. Offertory
19. Narrative of the Institution
20. The Thanksgiving
21. The Lord's Prayer
22. The Peace
23. The Breaking of the Bread and Pouring of the Wine
24. Agnus Dei
25. The Sharing of the Bread and Wine
26. Prayer after Communion
27. Nunc Dimittis
28. Concluding Praise
29. Dismissal
30. Blessing

1. Scripture Sentences (1a)

This is the day that the Lord has made;
Let us rejoice and be glad in it.
It is good to give thanks to the Lord
For his love endures forever.

Ps. 118: 24, 29

General

Our help is in the name of the Lord, maker of heaven and earth.
Ps. 124: 8

Christ our Passover has been sacrificed for us; therefore let us keep the feast. *1 Cor. 5: 7–8*

How can I repay the Lord for all his benefits toward me? I shall lift the cup of salvation and call on the name of the Lord.
Ps. 116: 12–13

Taste and see that the Lord is good. Happy are those who find refuge in him. *Ps. 34: 8*

Advent

It shall be said in that day, This is our God; we have waited for him, and he will save us. *Isa. 25: 9*

The glory of the Lord shall be revealed, and all flesh shall see it together, for the mouth of the Lord has spoken. *Isa. 40: 5*

Rain righteousness, you heavens, let the skies above pour down, let the earth open to receive it, that it may bear the fruit of salvation with righteousness in blossom at its side.

Isa. 45: 8

Christmas

Unto us a child is born, unto us a son is given. *Isa. 9: 6*

God is love; and his love was disclosed to us in this, that he sent his only Son into the world to bring us life. *1 John 4: 8–9*

Epiphany

The grace of God has dawned upon the world with healing for all people. *Titus 2: 11 (adapted)*

God was in Christ reconciling the world to himself, and has entrusted us with the message of reconciliation. *2 Cor. 5: 19*

Lent

Compassion and forgiveness belong to the Lord our God, though we have rebelled against him. *Dan. 9: 9*

Jesus said: If anyone would come after me, let them deny themselves, take up their cross, and follow me.
Mark 8: 34 (adapted)

Passiontide

Christ humbled himself, and in obedience accepted even death—death on a cross. *Phil. 2: 8*

Christ himself bore our sins in his body on the tree, that we might die to sin and live to righteousness. By his wounds we have been healed. *1 Pet. 2: 24*

Palm Sunday

Blessed is he who comes in the name of the Lord. Hosanna in the highest. *Mark 11: 9–10*

Easter

Christ is risen. He is risen indeed. Alleluia.

Thanks be to God! He gives us victory through our Lord Jesus Christ. *1 Cor. 15: 57*

Ascension

Lift up your heads, O you gates; and be lifted up, you everlasting doors; and the king of glory shall come in. *Ps. 24: 7*

The Lord reigns! Let the heavens be glad, and let the earth rejoice. *Ps. 96: 10–11*

Pentecost

God's love has been poured into our hearts through the Holy Spirit he has given us. *Rom. 5: 5*

Here is the proof that we dwell in God and God dwells in us: he has given his Spirit to us. *1 John 4: 13*

Trinity

Holy, holy, holy is God the sovereign Lord of all, who was, and is, and is to come! *Rev. 4: 8*

All Saints

Since we are surrounded by so great a cloud of witnesses, let us lay aside every weight, and the sin which clings so closely, and let us run with perseverance the race that is set before us, looking to Jesus the pioneer and perfecter of our faith. *Heb. 12: 1*

Harvest

To the Lord belong the earth and everything in it, the world and all its inhabitants. *Ps. 24: 1*

New Year

The Lord will guard you as you come and go, now and for evermore. *Ps. 121: 8*

2. Prayer of Approach (2a)

**Almighty God,
to whom all hearts are open,
all desires known,
and from whom no secrets are hidden:
cleanse the thoughts of our hearts
by the inspiration of your Holy Spirit,
that we may perfectly love you,
and worthily magnify your holy Name;
through Christ our Lord. Amen.**

or

Almighty God, (2b)
**infinite and eternal
in wisdom, power, and love:
we praise you for all that you are,
and for all that you do for the world.
You have shown us your truth and your love
in our Saviour Jesus Christ.
Help us by your Spirit
to worship you in spirit and in truth;
through Jesus Christ our Lord. Amen.**

or

You are holy, God the Creator, giving us richly all things to enjoy. You are holy, Christ the Saviour of the world, made flesh to set us free. You are holy, Spirit of truth and love, willing to dwell in us. You are holy and blessed, O God, eternal Trinity, and we worship you.

Amen

3. Confession of Sin

If we say we have no sin, we deceive ourselves. If we confess our sins, God is faithful and just and will forgive our sins and cleanse us from every kind of wrong.

Lord God most merciful, (3a)
we confess that we have sinned,
through our own fault,
and in common with others,
in thought, word, and deed,
and through what we have left undone.

We ask to be forgiven.

By the power of your Spirit
turn us from evil to good,
help us to forgive others,
and keep us in your ways
of righteousness and love;
through Jesus Christ our Lord. Amen.

or

I confess to God almighty and in the presence of all God's people that I have sinned in thought, word, and deed, and I pray God almighty to have mercy on me.

May almighty God have mercy on you, (3c)
pardon and deliver you from all your sins
and give you time to amend your life.

We confess to God almighty
and in the presence of all his people
that we have sinned in thought, word, and deed,
and we pray God almighty to have mercy on us.

May almighty God have mercy on you, pardon and deliver you from all your sins and give you time to amend your life.

or

O God, we confess as individuals, as a Church, and in common with all people, that we have disobeyed your commandments.

AN ORDER OF WORSHIP

We have not worshipped you, the only God, and we have not heeded your call to holy living.

**We have not loved you with all our heart
and soul and mind and strength.**

We have not discerned Christ:
we have hated when we should have loved,
broken when we should have healed;
we have divided the Church
and allowed our brothers and sisters to go hungry
while we have too much.

**We have not loved our neighbours as ourselves.
For all our sins we deserve your judgement
and we plead for your mercy;
through Christ our Lord. Amen.**

4. Assurance of Pardon (4a)

In repentance and in faith receive the promise of grace and the assurance of pardon:

Here are words you may trust, words that merit full acceptance: 'Christ Jesus came into the world to save sinners.'
To all who turn to him he says: 'Your sins are forgiven.' He also says: 'Follow me.'

Thanks be to God.

or (4b)

'God so loved the world that he gave his only Son, that everyone who has faith in him may not perish but have eternal life.'
To all who repent and believe, we declare in the name of the Father, the Son, and the Holy Spirit: God grants you the forgiveness of your sins.

Thanks be to God.

5. Kyries (5)

Here or in the prayer of confession

**Lord, have mercy.
Christ, have mercy.
Lord, have mercy.**

6. Gloria in Excelsis (6)

Glory to God in the highest,
and peace to God's people on earth.

Lord God, heavenly King,
almighty God and Father,
we worship you, we give you thanks,
we praise you for your glory.

Lord Jesus Christ, only Son of the Father,
Lord God, Lamb of God,
you take away the sin of the world:
   have mercy on us;
you are seated at the right hand of the Father:
   receive our prayer.

For you alone are the Holy One,
you alone are the Lord,
you alone are the Most High,
   Jesus Christ,
   with the Holy Spirit,
   in the glory of God the Father. Amen.

7. Prayer for Grace or Collect

THE MINISTRY OF THE WORD

8. **Theme Introduction**
9. **Old Testament Reading** (and/or New Testament Reading)
10. **Psalm, Canticle, or Anthem** (eg Alleluias)
11. **New Testament Reading** (or Readings: Epistle and Gospel)
12. **Sermon**
13. **Creed; Confession of Faith; or Prayer**
14. **Notices**
15. **Special Acts** (such as Baptism)
16. **Intercession** (if not in Thanksgiving Prayer)

AN ORDER OF WORSHIP
THE SACRAMENT OF THE LORD'S SUPPER

17. Invitation

Let us celebrate this joyful feast. People will come from east and west and north and south and sit at table in the kingdom of God.

Jesus said, I am the bread of life; whoever comes to me will never be hungry, and whoever believes in me will never be thirsty. Anyone who comes to me I will never turn away.

John 6: 35, 37

18. Offertory

Almighty and most merciful God, out of the fulness of your gifts we bring before you this bread and wine, our money, and our lives. Blessed be your holy name forever, through Jesus Christ our Lord.
Amen.

or

Blessed are you, Lord, God of all creation.
Through your goodness we have this bread to offer,
which earth has given and human hands have made.
It will become for us the bread of life.
Blessed be God forever.

Blessed are you, Lord, God of all creation.
Through your goodness we have this wine to offer,
fruit of the vine and the work of human hands.
It will become for us the cup of salvation.
Blessed be God forever.

Blessed are you, Lord, God of all creation.
Through your goodness we have ourselves to offer,
fruit of the womb, and formed by your love.
We will become your people for the world.
Blessed be God forever.

19. Narrative of the Institution (if not in the Thanksgiving Prayer)

Hear the narrative of the institution of the Lord's Supper as it was recorded by the Apostle Paul.

The tradition which I handed on to you came to me from the Lord himself: that on the night of his arrest the Lord Jesus took bread, and after giving thanks to God broke it and said: 'This is my body, which is for you; do this in memory of me.' In the same way, he took the cup after supper, and said: 'This cup is the new covenant sealed by my blood. Whenever you drink it, do this in memory of me.'

For every time you eat this bread and drink the cup, you proclaim the death of the Lord, until he comes.   *1 Cor. 11: 23–6*

or

A number of readers may be used in the following section.   **(11)**

During supper Jesus poured water into a basin, and began to wash his disciples' feet and to wipe them with a towel.
He said: 'If I do not wash you, you have no part with me.'

By that baptism into his death we were buried with Christ and lay dead,
so that as Christ was raised from death we might walk in new life.

Jesus said: 'How I have longed to eat this Passover with you before my death, for I will not eat it again until it is fulfilled in the kingdom of God.'

Christ our Passover has been sacrificed for us.
Therefore let us keep the feast.

As they were eating, he said: 'Truly I say to you, one of you will betray me.' And they were very sorrowful, and began to ask: 'Is it I?'

For I do not do what I want, but I do the very thing I hate.
Who will deliver me from this body of death?

Jesus took bread, blessed and broke it, and said: 'Take, eat; this

AN ORDER OF WORSHIP

is my body.' And he took a cup and said: 'Drink of it, all of you; for this is my blood of the covenant which is poured out for the forgiveness of sins.'

Ours is not a high priest unable to sympathize with our weaknesses, but one who has been tested in every way.
Therefore let us boldly approach the throne of God.

He said: 'You are those who have stood by me in my trials. I now give you the kingship which my Father gave me, and you shall eat and drink at my table in my kingdom.'

Blessed be the coming kingdom of our father David.
Peace in heaven and glory in the highest.

20. The Thanksgiving (12)

Thanksgiving I

Lift up your hearts.
We lift them to the Lord.
Let us give thanks to the Lord our God.
It is right to give our thanks and praise.

Holy and blessed are you, Lord our God,
King of the universe.
In the beginning you brought light out of darkness,
life out of clay.
When in Adam we disobeyed,
you did not cease loving us.
When we were slaves in Egypt,
you led us to freedom through the Red Sea.
When we wandered in the wilderness,
you gave us bread and revealed the Law to be our guide.
You brought us over Jordan to the promised land,
but we were unfaithful
and would not listen to your prophets.
Yet even in the bitterness of exile
and the harshness of oppression
your faithfulness has always surrounded us.
In the fulness of time, you sent your Son Jesus
to be the living bread and the fulfilment of the Law.

Born of Mary, baptized by John,
he lived among us and proclaimed your kingdom,
healed the sick, ate with outcasts,
bound up the brokenhearted, challenged the proud.
Yet he was betrayed, tortured, and crucified.
In anguish of spirit he opened his arms
and gave up his life.
But out of the depths you raised him up,
broke the power of the enemy,
and won for us forgiveness of our sins
by the power of his cross.
You exalted him as Lord of life
to reign with you eternally,
victorious over sin and death.

Seasonal prefaces may be included here—see page 17

Therefore with all your people in heaven and on earth we sing the triumphant hymn of your glory:

Holy, holy, holy Lord, (12)
God of power and might, **(Sung version: 13)**
Heaven and earth are full of your glory.
Hosanna in the highest.

Blessed is he who comes in the name of the Lord.

Hosanna in the highest.

[That we might keep this ever before us:
on the night he was betrayed
he came to table with his disciples,
washed their feet,
took bread, gave thanks,
broke it and said:
'Take, eat; this is my body.'

Likewise he took a cup, gave it to them and said:
'Drink of it, all of you, for this is my blood of the new covenant.
Do this in remembrance of me.'

Let us proclaim the mystery of faith: **(14)**

AN ORDER OF WORSHIP

Christ has died.
Christ is risen.
Christ will come again.]

Therefore remembering the work and passion
of our Saviour Christ,
and pleading his eternal sacrifice,
we set forth this memorial,
which he willed us to make.
Send down your Spirit upon these your gifts
that they may be for us his body and blood,
and in receiving them, we may be healed
and renewed to serve you in the world.

[We pray not only for ourselves but for your whole Church . . .
for the victims of torture, poverty, and war . . .
for those ill in body, mind, or heart . . .
Lord of the living and the dead,
remember those dear to us
and those who have died unloved and forgotten.]

Bring us together from east and west
and north and south
to sit with Abraham, Isaac, and Jacob,
(and . . . whom we remember this day)
so that at the wedding feast of the Lamb
we may rejoice with all the redeemed.
This we ask through Jesus Christ,
your Son, our Lord,
who with you, Father, and the Holy Spirit,
reigns now and forever.
Amen.

Thanksgiving II (12)

Lift up your hearts.
  We lift them to the Lord.
Let us give thanks to the Lord our God.
  It is right to give our thanks and praise.

With joy we give you thanks and praise,
almighty God, Source of all life and love,
that we live in your world,
that you are always
creating and sustaining it by your power,
and that you have so made us
that we can know and love you,
trust and serve you.

We give you thanks
that you loved the world so much
that you gave your only Son,
so that everyone who has faith in him
may not die but have eternal life.

Seasonal prefaces may be included here

Therefore with all your people in heaven and on earth we sing the triumphant hymn of your glory:

Holy, holy, holy Lord, (12) (**Sung version: 13**)
God of power and might,
heaven and earth are full of your glory.
Hosanna in the highest.

Blessed is he who comes in the name of the Lord.

Hosanna in the highest.

Holy Lord God,
by what we do here
in remembrance of Christ
we celebrate
   his perfect sacrifice on the cross
   and his glorious resurrection and ascension;
we declare
   that he is Lord of all;
and we prepare for
   his coming in his kingdom.
We pray that
through your Holy Spirit
this bread may be for us
the body of Christ
and this wine the blood of Christ.

Accept our sacrifice of praise;
and as we eat and drink at his command
unite us to Christ
as one body in him,
and give us strength to serve you in the world.

And to you, one holy and eternal God,
Father, Son, and Holy Spirit,
we give praise and glory, now and for ever.
Amen.

Thanksgiving III (12)

Lift up your hearts.
   We lift them to the Lord.
Let us give thanks to the Lord our God.
   It is right to give our thanks and praise.
It is indeed our joy,
to give you thanks always and everywhere,
our Creator and Redeemer, God of love and holiness.
In your image you made us all;
your universe you put into our care;
your creation you entrust to our hands,
with all its wonders and its travail.
You make us partners in your labours
and invite us to share in your peace.
We give you thanks that you so loved the world
that you gave your only Son,
that everyone who has faith in him
may not die but have eternal life.

Seasonal prefaces may be included here

Therefore with all your people in heaven and on earth we sing the triumphant hymn of your glory:

Holy, holy, holy Lord, (12) **(Sung version: 13)**
God of power and might,
heaven and earth are full of your glory.
Hosanna in the highest.

Blessed is he who comes in the name of the Lord.

Hosanna in the highest.

Lord, send on us
and on this thanksgiving meal the Spirit of life,
who spoke through Moses and the prophets,
who descended on Jesus at the river Jordan,
and on the apostles on the first day of Pentecost.
Send this same Spirit of fire
that its coming may transfigure our humanity
by the power of Christ's blood.
During supper, Jesus took bread,
and having said the blessing,
broke it and gave it to the disciples saying:
'Take, eat, this is my body.'
Then he took a cup
and, having given thanks,
he gave it to them, saying,
'This is my blood, the blood of the new covenant,
shed for the many, for the remission of sins.
Truly I declare to you,
I will never again drink of the fruit of the vine
until the day I drink it new in the kingdom of God.'

Let us proclaim the mystery of faith:

Christ has died.
Christ is risen.
Christ will come again.

As we celebrate before you
the memorial of the death and resurrection of your Son,
we offer you thanks, Lord,
for having chosen us to serve in your presence.

We pray that you will make us partakers
of Christ's body and blood
and unite us in a single body.
Grant that we, with Mary and the faithful of all times,
with Peter, Paul, and the other apostles,
may share in eternal life and sing your praises
through Jesus Christ, your beloved Son,

AN ORDER OF WORSHIP 17

Through him, with him, and in him, be all honour and glory to you, God the Father almighty, in the unity of the Holy Spirit, now and forever.
Amen.

SEASONAL PREFACES

Advent

We praise you that through his coming your promises given by the prophets were fulfilled, and the day of our deliverance has dawned; and, through him you will make all things new, as he comes in power and triumph to judge the world.

Christmas

We praise you that he took our nature and was born as the child of Mary, that he might share our life, reveal your love, reconcile us to yourself, and give us power to become your children.

Epiphany

We praise you that he is the Light of the World, through whom we are brought out of darkness into light, and that by him your glory is being revealed to the nations.

Lent

We praise you that, being made like us, he was tested every way yet without sin, and that having endured and overcome temptation, he is able to help us in our times of trial, and to give us strength to take up the cross and follow him.

Passiontide

We praise you that for us and for our salvation he humbled himself, obediently accepted even death—death on a cross; and that he bore our sins in his body on the tree, that we, being dead to sin, should live to righteousness.

Easter

We praise you that after he had suffered and been put to death on the cross, he was raised from the dead by your power; that he is the true Passover Lamb who takes away the sin of the world; and that by his glorious resurrection he has restored to us eternal life and given us the joy of your kingdom.

Ascension

We praise you that having suffered and died for us, and being raised from the dead, he lives and reigns for ever in your glory, and so fulfils his promise to be with us always, to the end of time.

Pentecost

We praise you that according to the promise of Christ, the Holy Spirit came to fill the Church with power, and still comes to us today, so that we being renewed and united in the Spirit, may be strong to proclaim the gospel in the world.

21. The Lord's Prayer

22. The Peace

The peace of the Lord be always with you.
Peace be with you.

The Peace may be shared
The Peace is sometimes shared before the offertory

23. The Breaking of the Bread and Pouring of the Wine

Christ our Passover is sacrificed for us.
Let us keep the feast.

The bread which we break is the communion of the body of Christ.

The cup of blessing which we bless is the communion of the blood of Christ.

24. Agnus Dei (14)

**Lamb of God, you take away the sin of the world,
  have mercy on us.
Lamb of God, you take away the sin of the world,
  have mercy on us.
Lamb of God, you take away the sin of the world,
  grant us peace.**

or

Jesus, Lamb of God: (15)
have mercy on us.
Jesus, bearer of our sins:
have mercy on us.
Jesus, redeemer of the world:
grant us peace.

and/or

Lord, I am not worthy to receive you, (17)
But only say the word and I shall be healed.

or

Behold the Lamb of God who takes away the sin of the world. Blessed are those who are called to the wedding feast of the Lamb.
Alleluia.

25. The Sharing of the Bread and Wine

Take, eat; this is the body of Christ broken for you. Do this in remembrance of him.

This cup is the new covenant in the blood of Christ, shed for you and for all, for the forgiveness of sin: drink of it.

or

The body of Christ, given for you.
The blood of Christ, shed for you.

or

The bread of heaven in Christ Jesus.
The cup of salvation in Christ Jesus.

26. Prayer After Communion

Accomplished and concluded, O Christ our Lord,
is the mystery which you have ordained.
For we have tasted your death,
seen your resurrection,
and have been filled with your unending life.

We have enjoyed your inexhaustible love,
through the grace of your eternal Father,
and the Holy Spirit, now and forever.
   Amen.

or

You have opened to us the scriptures O Christ,
and you have been known to us in the breaking of bread.
Stay with us, we pray,
that we may go with the strength of your presence
all our journey through, *(as our story unfolds)*
and at its end behold you
in the glory of the eternal Trinity,
God for ever and ever.
   Amen.

or

Father of all, we give you thanks and praise,
that when we were still far off
you met us in your Son and brought us home.
Dying and living, he declared your love,
gave us grace, and opened the gate of glory.
May we who share Christ's body live his risen life;
we who drink his cup bring life to others;
we whom the Spirit lights give light to the world.
Keep us firm in the hope you have set before us;
so that we and all your children may be free,
and the whole earth live to praise your name;
through Christ our Lord.
   Amen.

or

Most gracious God,
we praise you for what you have given
and for what you have promised us here.
You have made us one
with all your people
in heaven and on earth.
You have fed us

with the bread of life,
and renewed us for your service.
Now we give ourselves to you;
and we ask that our daily living
may be part of the life of your kingdom,
and that our love may be your love
reaching out into the life of the world;
through Jesus Christ our Lord.
   Amen.

27. Nunc Dimittis (18)

Now, Lord let your servant go in peace:
your word has been fulfilled.
My own eyes have seen the salvation
which you have prepared in the sight of every people:
a light to reveal you to the nations,
and the glory of your people Israel.
Glory to the Father, and to the Son,
   and to the Holy Spirit:
as it was in the beginning, is now,
   and will be for ever. Amen.

Luke 2: 29–32

28. The Concluding Praise (19)

Give thanks to the Lord for he is good,
   for his love endures forever.
Let those who fear the Lord say,
   his love endures forever.
Out of the depths I called upon the Lord;
   he answered and freed me.
The Lord is at my side; I do not fear.
   What can they do against me?
The Lord's right hand has triumphed;
   we shall not die, we shall live
   to proclaim the works of the Lord.
The stone which the builders rejected
has become the chief corner-stone.

**This is the work of the Lord,
a marvel in our eyes.**
We bless you from the house of the Lord.
My God, I praise you.
Give thanks to the Lord for he is good,
for his love endures forever.

29. Dismissal

Go in peace to love and serve the Lord.

or

Go out into the world with the food of your pilgrimage in peace and gladness.

30. Blessing

And the blessing of God almighty,
the Father, the Son, and the Holy Spirit,
be with you always.
Amen. (20)

SECOND ORDER OF WORSHIP

1. Scripture Sentences
2. Prayer, Confession, and Assurance of Pardon*
3. Scripture Readings*
4. Sermon
5. Open or Responsive Prayers of Thanksgiving and Intercession: The Lord's Prayer
6. The Peace
7. Offertory
8. The Approach to Communion*
9. Narrative of the Institution*
10. Thanksgiving and Sharing
11. Prayer after Communion*
12. Blessing*

* indicates that these parts of the service need to be used in taking communion with the sick and the housebound.

This order allows for considerable flexibility and variation according to circumstances. The opening sentences may be said responsively and other responses may be used in the service. Seasonal sentences may be used at the beginning of the service; hymns may be introduced as appropriate; alternative prayers and canticles, and/or silence may also be used. Provision is made for open prayers of thanksgiving and intercession to be led spontaneously by members of the congregation. There should always be a brief exposition of the reading(s) from Scripture, related to the circumstances of the congregation, even if a full sermon has to be omitted.

SECOND ORDER OF WORSHIP

1. Scripture Sentences

Give thanks to the God of heaven, (1b)
   for his love endures for ever. *Ps. 136: 26*

The stone which the builders rejected
   has become the main corner-stone.
This is the work of the Lord;
   it is wonderful in our eyes. *Ps. 118: 22–3*

2. Prayer, Confession, and Assurance of Pardon

Eternal God, creator of all things, giver of life,
we praise and worship you.
We thank you that you have
always loved the world you have made;
and that, however far we stray from you,
your love is always there to welcome us home.

We do not deserve your love,
but we dare to believe the good news of your mercy
declared by our Lord Jesus Christ,
whose offering of his life for us and for all people
we set forth in this bread and wine.

Be present at this your table
as with penitent and forgiving hearts,
we break bread and drink wine in your name.
Fill us with your Holy Spirit,
that our worship may truly express our love
for you and for one another.
Make us glad and give us joy and peace.

Let us confess our sins:

God our Father, (3b)
we have sinned against you and against one another,
in thought, word, and deed;
we have not loved you with all our heart;
we have not loved our neighbour as ourselves.
But you have kept faith with us.
Have mercy on us,

**forgive us our sins,
and restore us to newness of life;
through Jesus Christ our Lord. Amen.**

Christ Jesus came into the world to save sinners.
To all who turn to him he says: 'Your sins are
forgiven.' He also says: 'Follow me.'

For strength to follow him, we listen to his word and gather round his table.

3. Scripture Readings

Old Testament; Epistle; Gospel.

4. Sermon

5. Open or Responsive Prayers of Thanksgiving and Intercession: The Lord's Prayer

6. The Peace

The peace of the Lord be always with you.
Peace be with you.

The Peace may be shared

7. Offertory (10a)

**Lord God, we bring to you the ordinary things of life—
food and drink and money—
and with them we bring ourselves.
Take us, and our gifts of money, to do your work in the world.
Take this food and drink from our tables
and feed us from your table with your love.
Accept the praise we offer;
through Jesus Christ our Lord.
Amen.**

or

Eternal God, (10b)
we come with these gifts
to offer the praise of our lips
and the service of our lives;
through Jesus Christ our Lord.
Amen.

8. The Approach to Communion

As we gather at this table, we remember
that Jesus was born of Mary;
he lived our common life on earth;
he suffered and died for us;
on the third day he rose again;
and he is always present through the Holy Spirit.
In his presence,
and in the company of all the people of God,
past, present, and to come,
we celebrate the Supper of the Lord.

'Behold, I stand at the door and knock; if anyone hears my voice and opens the door, I will come in to him and eat with him, and he with me.'

Rev. 3: 20

or

How shall I repay the Lord for all his benefits to me?
I will take the cup of salvation,
and call upon the name of the Lord.
I will offer you a sacrifice of thanksgiving,
and call upon the name of the Lord.

Ps. 116: 11–12; 16

or

Blessed are those who hunger and thirst to see right prevail for they shall be satisfied.

Matt. 5: 6

9. Narrative of the Institution

Hear again the words of institution of this feast as they are given by the Apostle Paul:

For I received from the Lord what I delivered to you, that the Lord Jesus on the night when he was betrayed took bread, and when he had given thanks, he broke it, and said, 'This is my body which is for you. Do this in remembrance of me.'

In the same way also he took the cup, after supper, saying 'This cup is the new covenant in my blood. Do this, as often as you drink it, in remembrance of me.'

For as often as you eat this bread and drink the cup, you proclaim the Lord's death until he comes.

I Cor. 11: 23–6

10. Thanksgiving and Sharing

Lift up your hearts. (12)
We lift them to the Lord.
Let us give thanks to the Lord our God.
It is right to give our thanks and praise.

We give thanks to you, O God,
that from the earth you cause the grain to come
for the making of bread.
We praise you for Christ, the bread of life,
whose body was broken for us.
By your Holy Spirit sanctify us and this loaf,
that the bread which we break may be to us
the communion of the body of Christ,
and that we may be made one in him.
As of old you fed your people in the wilderness,
so feed us now that we may live to your praise;
through Jesus Christ our Lord.
Amen.

The minister breaks the bread saying:

When Jesus had given thanks,
he broke the bread and said:
'Take, eat: this is my body which is given for you.
Do this in remembrance of me.'

The distribution takes place

We give thanks to you, O God,
that you cause the vine to yield fruit.
We bless you for Christ, the true vine,
whose blood was poured out for us.
By your Holy Spirit sanctify us and this wine,
that the cup which we bless may be to us
the communion of the blood of Christ,
and that through abiding in him
we may bear fruit that shall last.
As we share the sufferings of Christ, so give us grace
that we may know the power of his resurrection;
through Jesus Christ our Lord.
   Amen.

The minister pours the wine and distributes it saying:

When Jesus had given thanks,
he gave the cup to his disciples and said:
'Drink this, all of you;
for this is my blood of the new covenant,
which is shed for you and for many,
for the forgiveness of sins.
Do this, as often as you drink it in
remembrance of me.'

or

Lift up your hearts. (12)
   We lift them to the Lord.
Let us give thanks to the Lord our God.
   It is right to give thanks and praise.

We give thanks to you, O God,
that from the earth you cause the grain to come
for the making of bread

and that you cause the vine to yield fruit.
We praise you for Christ,
the bread of life and true vine,
whose body was broken for us,
and whose blood was poured out for us.

By your Holy Spirit sanctify us and these your gifts
of bread and wine,
that the bread which we break
may be the communion of the body of Christ,
and the cup which we bless
may be the communion of the blood of Christ.
give us grace to share his sufferings
and to know the power of his resurrection,
that we may be made one and evermore abide in him,
to your praise and glory;
through Jesus Christ our Lord.
Amen.

The minister breaks the bread saying:

When Jesus had given thanks he broke the bread and said:
'Take, eat: this is my body which is for you.
Do this in remembrance of me.'

The distribution takes place

The minister pours the wine and distributes it saying:

When Jesus had given thanks,
he gave the cup to his disciples and said:
'Drink this, all of you;
for this is my blood of the new covenant,
which is shed for you and for many,
for the forgiveness of sins.
Do this, as often as you drink it, in remembrance of me.'

11. Prayer After Communion

Strengthen for service, Lord,
the hands that have taken holy things.
May the ears that have heard your word
be deaf to clamour and dispute.

May the eyes that have seen your great love
shine with the light of hope.
May the tongues that have sung your praise
also speak the truth.
May the feet that have walked in your house
ever walk in the light.
May the bodies that have tasted your living body be
restored to newness of life.
Thanks be to God for his gift beyond words.
   Amen.

or

Nunc Dimittis (18)

**Now, Lord let your servant go in peace:
your word has been fulfilled.
My own eyes have seen the salvation
which you have prepared in the sight of every people:
a light to reveal you to the nations,
and the glory of your people Israel.
Glory to the Father, and to the Son,
   and to the Holy Spirit:
as it was in the beginning, is now,
   and will be for ever. Amen.**   *Luke 2: 29–32*

12. Blessing **(Sung Amens: 20)**

BAPTISM SERVICE

1. Introduction
2. The Promises
3. The Baptismal Prayer
4. The Baptism
5. Prayer

1. Introduction

We now celebrate the Sacrament of Baptism in which God has called *A* . . . to be a member of Christ's body. At the beginning of his ministry Jesus was baptized by John in the Jordan. The Spirit descended upon him and a voice came from heaven: 'This is my beloved Son on whom my favour rests.' His baptism found fulfilment in the cross where he gave himself for the life of the world. When God raised him from the dead, he said to his disciples:

'Full authority in heaven and on earth has been committed to me. Go therefore to all nations and make them my disciples; baptize them in the name of the Father and of the Son and of the Holy Spirit: teach them to observe all that I have commanded you. I will be with you always, to the end of time.'

Matt. 28: 19–20

On the day of Pentecost Peter said to the people:

'Repent, and be baptized every one of you in the name of Jesus Christ for the forgiveness of your sins; and you shall receive the gift of the Holy Spirit. For the promise is to you and to your children and to all that are far off, every one whom the Lord our God calls to him.'

Acts 2: 38–39

Baptism unites us to Christ and to all that God accomplishes for all people and all time. In baptism we are buried with Christ and are raised with him to new life; our sins are washed away, and we are brought into the covenant of grace; we receive the Spirit to equip us as members of Christ's body, the Church.

2. The Promises

A . . . you have come for baptism in response to the call of Christ and the leading of the Holy Spirit. Let us hear, then, in the presence of God and before us as witnesses, that you confess your faith in Christ and promise to follow him. As a congregation we will also make our promises.

To the candidate in believer's baptism

Do you believe and trust in one God, Father, Son, and Holy Spirit,
maker of heaven and earth,
redeemer of the world,
giver of life?
  I do.

Do you, trusting in God's grace,
repent of your sins,
renounce evil, and turn to Christ?
  I do.

Do you promise,
trusting in God's grace,
to be faithful in public
and private worship,
to live in the fellowship
of the Church
and to share in its witness.
  I do.

Do you promise,
by that same grace,
to follow Christ
and to seek to do
and to bear his will
all the days of your life?
  I do

The Promises

N . . . you have come for the baptism of your child in response to the call of Christ and the leading of the Holy Spirit. Let us hear, then, in the presence of God, and before us as witnesses, that you confess your faith in Christ and promise to follow him. As a congregation we will also make our promises.

To parents (and sponsors) in infant baptism

Do you believe and trust in one God, Father, Son and Holy Spirit,
maker of heaven and earth,
redeemer of the world,
giver of life?
  I do.

To parents in infant baptism:

Do you promise,
trusting in God's grace,
that by prayer and example
you will teach A . . .
the faith of the gospel
and bring *him/her* up
in the worship and life
of the Church?
  I do.

To sponsors:

Do you promise,
trusting in God's grace,
to pray and care for A . . .
and support *his/her* family
as you are able?
  I do.

And do you trust
in his mercy alone
to bring you into the fullness of
the life of the world to come?
I do.

To the congregation:

Do you, as members of Christ's body and trusting in God's grace, promise to pray for *A* . . ., provide for the teaching of the gospel, and live a Christian life in the family of God?
We do.

3. The Baptismal Prayer

Almighty God,
through water you bring us bountiful love.
In the beginning
your Spirit moved over the face of the waters
bringing order out of chaos;
with the waters of the flood
you cleansed the world,
and through the Red Sea and across the Jordan
you led your people to the land of promise.
By the life and death of your Son
and by his mighty resurrection and ascension
you have given us the assurance
that healing waters will flow from him for all nations.

We pray that *A* . . ., who is washed in this water,
may be made one with Christ in his death,
cleansed from all sin
and delivered from all evil.

Send your Holy Spirit upon *A* . . .
for new birth in the family of your Church,
and raise *him/her* with Christ to full and eternal life.
For all might, majesty, authority, and power
are yours, now and forever.
Amen.

or

Almighty and eternal God
we give you thanks
for our life and salvation in Jesus your Son,
who became one with us
and died and rose again,
so that we might have life in him,
be made members of your Church
and heirs of your kingdom.
Be with us in the power of your Spirit,
and so use this water and our obedience to Christ,
that *A* . . . whom we baptize in your name,
may receive the fullness of your grace
and always remain in the number of your faithful people;
through Jesus Christ our Lord.
Amen.

4. The Baptism

A . . ., I baptize you in the name of the Father, the Son, and the Holy Spirit.
Amen.

May the Lord bless you and take care of you;
May the Lord be kind and gracious to you;
May the Lord look on you with favour
and give you peace.

or

The Lord bless you and keep you;
the Lord make his face to shine upon you
and be gracious unto you;
the Lord lift up his countenance upon you
and give you peace. Amen. *Num. 6: 24–6*

A lighted candle may be given

This is to show that you have received the light of Christ. Shine as a light in the world to the glory of God the Father.

You are witnesses that *A* . . . has been received into the household of God, the one, holy, catholic, and apostolic Church.

He/she belongs to a chosen race, a royal priesthood, a holy nation, God's own people.

For believer's baptism

The Minister lays his/her hand on the head of the candidate and says:

A . . ., the God of all grace, who has called you to Christian faith and service, confirm and strengthen you with the Holy Spirit and keep you faithful to Christ all your days.
  Amen.

In the name of the Lord Jesus Christ and in accordance with the decision of this church, we welcome you to the membership of this congregation with its privileges and responsibilities. May your joining be a blessing to you and to all of us and may our one Lord keep us one with all his people, for ever.
  Amen.

The right hand of fellowship is given.

5. Prayer

Almighty God, we give you thanks for A . . ., who has been baptized today, for the grace of your acceptance and the promise of resurrection. Uphold and strengthen *him/her* for your service and keep *him/her* always true to Christ.

For infant baptism

5. Prayer

Heavenly Father, we give thanks for receiving this little child by baptism into the life of your Church. Keep *him/her* always in your love; grant that *he/she* may grow strong in body and in mind; protect *him/her* in all dangers and temptations; and bring *him/her* to faith in Jesus Christ as Saviour and Lord.

We ask your blessing on the parents, family, and friends of this child. Help them to surround *him/her* with love and security, give them grace and wisdom to teach your truth and your way. Through their love for this child may they learn to love you more. We commend to you their home and all the families of this congregation.

Grant that in our homes we may honour you and love and serve each other. Accept us as we recall our own baptism and rededicate ourselves to you; and help us to care for all who are one with us in the life of your Church; through Jesus Christ our Lord.
  Amen.

Let your blessing rest continually upon us all so that we who have been called to enter your kingdom, may now and always be found faithful; through Jesus Christ our Lord.
Amen.

THANKSGIVING FOR THE BIRTH OF A CHILD

The Dedication of Parents and the Blessing of Children

1. Introduction
2. The Word
3. Thanksgiving, Dedication, and Blessing
4. Prayers

This act is intended for parents who are church members and who, on the grounds of belief, do not wish to have their children baptized; and also for those parents who are not able in conscience to make the promise required at the baptism of infants. In either case the act looks forward to baptism at a point in the future, and is not therefore a substitute for baptism.

The act may take place at any suitable point within worship but congregations will probably wish to have it when other children are present.

When only one parent is present the wording of the service will need to be adapted.

1. Introduction

It is good to give thanks to the Lord
for his love endures for ever. *Ps. 106: 1*

My soul shall live for him, my children serve him.
They shall tell of the Lord to the coming generations,
and proclaim his deliverance to people yet unborn:
These things the Lord has done. *Ps. 22: 30–1 (adapted)*

We are gathered together, as on each Lord's Day, as part of the family of God. Today we welcome A and C who have come to give thanks to God for the birth of their *son/daughter* N . . ., to seek God's blessing upon *him/her*, and to dedicate themselves (again) to the high task of parenthood.

We share in their thanksgiving. We acknowledge the claim of this child upon the prayers and support of the church both now and in the years ahead.

We welcome *him/her* as Jesus Christ welcomed children. And we affirm that it is the duty of parents and of the church together so to show the love of God in their lives, that in due time this child may come to confess *his/her* faith in Jesus Christ and be baptized.

2. The Word

We read in the Old Testament:

Hear, O Israel, the Lord our God is one Lord; and you shall love the Lord your God with all your heart, and with all your soul, and with all your might. And these words which I command you this day shall be upon your heart; and you shall teach them diligently to your children, and shall talk of them when you sit in your house, and when you walk by the way, and when you lie down, and when you rise. *Deut. 6: 4–7*

Further, we read in the Gospels:

They brought children for Jesus to touch. The disciples rebuked them, but when Jesus saw this he was indignant, and said to them: 'Let the children come to me; do not try to stop them; for the kingdom of God belongs to such as these. I tell you, whoever does not accept the kingdom of God like a child will never enter it.' And he put his arms round them, laid his hands upon them, and blessed them.

Mark 10: 13–16

3. Thanksgiving, Dedication, and Blessing

For church members

A and *C*, do you thank God for the gift of this child, and commit yourselves to God in fulfilling the responsibilities of parenthood?

We do.

Do you promise, by God's grace, to provide a Christian home for this child, and to bring *him/her* up in the faith of the Gospel and the fellowship of the church?

We do.

THANKSGIVING FOR THE BIRTH OF A CHILD

And do you promise, by God's grace, so to live that your child will be nurtured through the years in Christian love?

We do.

or

For parents who are not church members

Do you promise, by God's grace, so to live that your child will be surrounded by love and goodness?

We do.

If there are older children in the family the minister may incorporate a suitable promise for them to make.

May the Lord give you grace faithfully to carry out the promises you have made this day: may he grant you joy and patience, love and peace.

The minister or one of the elders says:

We as a congregation, and on behalf of the whole Church of Jesus Christ, undertake to provide for the instruction of this child in the Gospel of God's love, the example of Christian faith and character, and the strong support of the family of God in prayer and friendship.

The minister or elder may give a Bible to the parents with an appropriate word of presentation

Then the minister, laying one hand upon the child's head and pronouncing his/her name, says:

N . . . the blessing of God Almighty, the Father, the Son, and the Holy Spirit, be with you, now and always.

Amen.

or

N . . . the Lord bless you and keep you;
the Lord make his face to shine upon you
and be gracious to you;
the Lord lift up his countenance upon you
and give you peace.

Amen. *Num. 6: 24–6*

If the minister does not use the Aaronic blessing, it may be sung by the congregation

4. Prayers

The Lord's Prayer may now be said.

O God, the Father of all, we thank you for the gift of this child. We thank you for the love that prepared for *his/her* coming and welcomed *him/her* into the world, and we rejoice with these parents in their hopes for the future. Be with them in their home. Guide them in the Christian upbringing of their child, and give them ever deeper knowledge and love of Christ.

Give us grace so to live that they and their family may find in the Christian fellowship a source of strength and love.

O God, we commend this child to your care. Give *him/her* health of body and mind. And in due time, may *he/she* come to be baptized, make *his/her* own profession of faith, and commit *his/her* life to Christ as *his/her* Saviour and Lord. So may *he/she* serve you, and come, with us, to share the joys of your eternal kingdom; through Jesus Christ our Lord.

Amen.

CONFIRMATION SERVICE

1. Introduction
2. Act of Witness
3. The Renewal of Baptismal Promises
4. The Confirmation
5. The Welcome

For those baptized at some time in the past who come to make their own confession of Christian faith and enter into the full privileges and responsibilities of membership of Christ's Church.

1. Introduction

In the name of the Lord Jesus Christ, the only head of the Church, we seek now the gift of the Holy Spirit in confirming and strengthening the faith of *ABC* . . .

In baptism we are welcomed into the family and household of God, raised to new life in Christ, and nurtured in the Holy Spirit. In response to the call of Christ and the leading of the Holy Spirit *ABC* . . . come(s) now to make *his/her/their* own profession of Christian faith, and to accept the responsibilities and privileges of membership.

2. Act of Witness

One or more candidates may bear witness to their faith in Christ.

3. The Renewal of Baptismal Promises

ABC . . . will now make *his/her/their* own the promises declared when *he was/she was, they were* baptized.

The congregation may be invited to share in making the promises as an act of renewal.

Do you believe and trust in one God,
Father, Son, and Holy Spirit,
maker of heaven and earth,

redeemer of the world,
giver of life?
   I do.

Do you, trusting in God's grace, repent of your sins, renounce evil, and turn to Christ?
   I do.

Do you promise, trusting in God's grace, to be faithful in public and private worship, to live in the fellowship of the Church, to share in its witness.
   I do.

Do you promise, by that same grace,
to follow Christ and to seek to do and to bear his will
all the days of your life?
   I do.

And do you trust in his mercy alone
to bring you into the fullness of the life of the world to come?
   I do.

4. The Confirmation

Almighty and ever-living God, by baptism you have delivered *ABC* . . . from the domain of darkness and brought *him/her/them* into the kingdom of your beloved Son, in whom our release is secured and our sins forgiven.

Send your Holy Spirit upon *him/her/them*: the spirit of wisdom and understanding; the spirit of counsel and power; the spirit of knowledge and the fear of the Lord.

The minister and elders lay hands on each candidate.

By your holy spirit confirm and strengthen, Lord, your servant *A* . . . *(candidate)*.
   Amen.

or

The God of all grace,
who has called you to Christian faith and service,

confirm and strengthen you with the Holy Spirit
and keep you faithful to Christ all your days.
Amen.

Peace be with you

Candidate(s): **And also with you**

Defend, Lord, your servant(s) with your heavenly grace, that *he/she/they* may continue to be yours for ever, bearing in life the fruits of the Spirit and growing into the full stature of Christ.
Amen.

5. The Welcome

In the name of the Lord Jesus Christ, and in accordance with the decision of the church meeting, I declare you to be admitted to the full privileges and responsibilities of membership of the one, holy, catholic, and apostolic Church, and in particular to the exercise of that membership in this congregation of Christ's people.

The minister and one or more of the elders give to the member(s) a sign of welcome (e.g. the kiss of peace or the right hand of fellowship). A Bible may be presented.

In the name of Christ we welcome you. May we grow together in unity, and be built up into the body of Christ in love, to the glory of God, Father, Son, and Holy Spirit, now and for ever.
Amen.

RENEWAL OF BAPTISMAL PROMISES

For use at services other than Confirmation.

1. Introduction
2. The Promises
3. Prayer
4. Blessing

1. Introduction

By baptism as infants we were welcomed into the family and household of God, and engaged to be the Lord's. By baptism as believers or at confirmation, we made our own profession of Christian faith, and accepted for ourselves the privileges and responsibilities of church membership. We come now together as the community of God's people at . . . . to renew the decision and promises we made then, and to rededicate ourselves to the service of God.

2. The Promises

Do you confess anew your faith in one God, Father, Son, and Holy Spirit,
maker of heaven and earth,
redeemer of the world,
giver of life?
   We do.

Do you, trusting in God's grace, repent of your sins, renounce evil, and turn to Christ?
   We do.

Do you promise,
trusting in God's grace,
to be faithful in public

and private worship,
to live in the fellowship of the church and to share in its witness?
  We do.

Do you promise,
by that same grace,
to follow Christ
and to seek to do
and to bear his will
all the days of your life?
  I do

And do you trust
in his mercy alone
to bring you into the fullness
of the life of the world to come?
  We do.

3. Prayer

A prayer such as the following may be suitable

Gracious God, you have called us into the service of your kingdom, and you equip us for our different tasks. Give us, your servants, who have rededicated ourselves to you the grace and power of the Holy Spirit, that we may be strengthened in faith, love and unity; through Jesus Christ our Lord.
  Amen.

4. Blessing

The God of all grace, who has called you to Christian faith and service, strengthen you with the Holy Spirit, and keep you faithful to Christ all your days.
  Amen.

RECEPTION OF MEMBERS FROM OTHER CHURCHES

1. Introduction
2. The Affirmation
3. The Welcome

1. Introduction

In the name of the Lord Jesus Christ, the only head of the church, and in accordance with the decision of the church, we now receive *A . . . B . . . C . . .*
according to circumstances
{ by transfer from *XYZ* church
{ by reaffirmation of faith
into membership of this congregation of the United Reformed Church.

2. The Affirmation

Let us now hear the affirmation that, trusting in the grace of God, *he/she/they* intend(s) to live as *a faithful member/faithful members* of this fellowship.

Do you confess anew your faith and trust in one God, Father, Son, and Holy Spirit, maker of heaven and earth, redeemer of the world, giver of life?
  I do.

Do you promise, trusting in God's grace, to be faithful in public and private worship, to live in the fellowship of the church, and to share in its witness?
  I do.

or

A . . ., do you confess anew your faith in one God, Father, Son, and Holy Spirit, promise to share with us in the life of this church, and to be faithful in the duties of membership?

I do.

3. The Welcome

The minister and one or more of the elders give to the new member(s) a sign of welcome (e.g. the kiss of peace or the right hand of fellowship). The minister says:

In the name of the Lord Jesus Christ, welcome.

The congregation may say:

**In the name of Christ we welcome you.
May we grow together in unity,
and be built up into the body of Christ in love,
to the glory of God, Father, Son, and Holy Spirit,
now and for ever. Amen.**

WEDDING SERVICE

1. Welcome
2. Scripture Sentences
3. Prayer of Approach
4. Hymn
5. The Purpose of Marriage
6. Legal Declarations
7. Prayer for Assurance and Sincerity
8. The Promises
9. The Vows
10. The Giving of the Ring or Rings
11. The Declaration
12. The Marriage Blessing
13. Greetings
14. Hymn
15. Scripture Reading(s) and Sermon
16. Prayers
17. Hymn
18. Blessing

Statements and responses may be made from memory, repeated after the minister, or read from the book or a printed order.

1. Welcome

The minister may greet and welcome the congregation, saying or concluding:

Grace to you and peace
from God our Father and the Lord Jesus Christ.

2. Scripture Sentences

The congregation is called to worship with one or more scripture sentences:

Let us worship God.

O give thanks to the Lord, for he is good;
his steadfast love endures for ever. *Ps. 106: 1*

This is the day that the Lord has made;
let us rejoice and be glad in it. *Ps. 118: 24*

God created human beings in his own image;
in the image of God he created them;
male and female he created them. *Gen. 1: 27*

Many waters cannot quench love,
no flood can sweep it away. *Song of Solomon 8: 7*

Dear friends, let us love one another,
because love is from God.
Everyone who loves is a child of God
and knows God. *1 John 4: 7*

God is love,
and those who live in love live in God,
and God lives in them. *1 John 4: 16*
(adapted)

3. Prayer of Approach (2)

Almighty God, to whom all hearts are open,
all desires known, and from whom no secrets are hidden;
cleanse the thoughts of our hearts by the inspiration
of your Holy Spirit, that we may perfectly love you,
and worthily magnify your holy name; through Christ
our Lord. Amen.

or

O God, your gracious love surrounds us,
and everything we enjoy comes from you.
We confess our ingratitude for your goodness
and our selfishness in the use of your gifts.
We ask you to forgive us
and to fill us with your Spirit,
that we may worship you now with free and open hearts,
and serve you always with thankful and generous lives;
through Jesus Christ our Lord.
Amen.

and/or

Gracious God, always faithful in your love for us,
we rejoice in your presence.
You create love
and out of loneliness
unite us in one human family.
You offer your word
and lead us in your light.
You open your loving arms and embrace us with strength.
May the presence of Christ fill our hearts
with new joy
and make new the lives
of *A* . . . and *B* . . . whose marriage we celebrate.
Bless all creation
through the sign of your love
given in their love for each other.
May the power of your Holy Spirit
sustain them and us,
in the love that knows no end.
   Amen.

4. Hymn

5. The Purpose of Marriage

We are gathered here in the presence of God
to celebrate the wedding of *AB* and *CD*,
to rejoice with them,
and to support them with our prayers.

Marriage is a gift and calling of God,
and is not to be entered upon lightly or thoughtlessly,
but reverently and responsibly,
in obedience to the gospel of Christ.

God has given us marriage so that husband and wife
may find comfort and companionship in each other,
and live faithfully together for the whole of their lives.

God has given us marriage so that husband and wife
may love and honour each other,
enrich and encourage each other,
and know each other with tenderness and joy.

God has given us marriage for the birth and nurture
of children, so that they may grow up in
the security of love, and come to experience
the freedom of faith.

God has given us marriage so that husband and wife,
being joined together as Christ with his Church,
may be a sign of unity and mutual commitment,
for the enrichment of society and the
strengthening of community.

This is the way of life that *A* . . . and *C* . . . are now to begin.
They come to give themselves freely to each other, to exchange
solemn promises, and to ask God's blessing
on their new life together.

The minister may say to the congregation:

If any know of any reason why *A* . . . and *C* . . . may not lawfully be married to each other, let them now declare it.

or

Due notice of their intention has been given, and no objection has been made.

6. Legal Declarations

(where required by law)

I now ask you both to say that you know of no reason why you may not lawfully be married.

The man says in the presence of the Authorized Person or the Registrar, and two witnesses, as required by law:

**I do solemnly declare
that I know not
of any lawful impediment
why I, *AB*,**

**may not be joined in matrimony
to *CD*.**

The woman says in the presence of the same persons, as required by law:

**I do solemnly declare
that I know not
of any lawful impediment
why I, *CD*,
may not be joined in matrimony
to *AB*.**

The scripture reading(s) may be taken now and a sermon preached, or they may be deferred until after the Marriage Blessing. See list of readings appended to this service.

7. Prayer for Assurance and Sincerity

God of love, ever gracious and ever kind,
we pray for *A* and *C* as they take the vows of marriage.
In repentance and in faith may they know you
as a God of mercy and new beginnings,
who forgives our failures,
restores our wholeness,
and renews our hope.
God of love, ever present and ever faithful,
may *A* and *C* be conscious that their marriage
is both your will and your delight.
May the promises they make govern the life they will lead.
May your presence surround them,
your faithfulness encourage them,
and your Spirit strengthen and guide them:
through Jesus Christ our Lord.
   Amen.

8. The Promises

A, will you take *C* to be your wife in Christian marriage?
Will you love her, comfort her,
honour and protect her,
in times of prosperity and health,
and in times of trouble and suffering,
and be faithful to her
as long as you both shall live?
   I will.

C, will you take *A* to be your husband in Christian marriage?
Will you love him, comfort him,
honour and protect him,
in times of prosperity and health,
and in times of trouble and suffering,
and be faithful to him
as long as you both shall live?
   I will.

In appropriate circumstances the parents of A *and* C, *and/or members of their families, and/or any children who will share in the new family, may be invited to stand and make the following promise:*

Do you . . ., give your blessing to this marriage of *A* and *C*, and promise always to support and encourage them?
   We do.

or the minister may say: 'Who gives this woman to be married to this man?' to which the response is: 'I do.'

When there are children who will share in the new family the minister may say:

A and *C*, will you be faithful, caring, and loving parents?
   We will.

The congregation may then be invited to make the promise:

And do you, as friends of *A* and *C*, promise to support and encourage them in their marriage?
   We do.

WEDDING SERVICE

9. The Vows

The bridegroom and bride turn to face each other and join their right hands. The man then says to the woman in the presence of the Authorized Person (or the Registrar) and two witnesses:

I call upon these persons here present
to witness that I, *AB*,
do take thee, *CD*,
to be my lawful wedded wife:*
in accordance with God's holy will,
to have and to hold
from this day forward,
for better, for worse,
for richer, for poorer,
in sickness and in health,
to love and to cherish
till death us do part.
This is my faithful promise.

The woman then says to the man in the presence of the same persons:

I call upon these persons here present
to witness that I, *CD*,
do take thee, *AB*,
to be my lawful wedded husband:*
in accordance with God's holy will,
to have and to hold
from this day forward,
for better, for worse,
for richer, for poorer,
in sickness and in health,
to love and to cherish
till death us do part.
This is my faithful promise.

**The following shorter form of legal declaration may be used when the Authorized Person is present but not when the Registrar attends:*

I, *AB*, do take thee, *CD*,
to be my wedded wife/husband.

10. The Giving of the Ring or Rings

God our Father, from all eternity you love us;
Lord Jesus Christ,
in love you came among us;
Holy Spirit,
you gave us love as your greatest gift.
Bless the giving and receiving of *this ring/these rings*, symbol(s) of unending love and faithfulness and reminder(s) of the promises made this day. We ask it for your love's sake.
Amen.

The following forms of words may be used at the exchange of the ring(s)

I give you this ring as a sign of our marriage. With my body I honour you, all that I am I give to you, and all that I have I share with you, within the love of God, Father, Son, and Holy Spirit.

or

I give you this ring in God's name as a symbol of all that we have promised and all that we shall share.

I receive this ring in God's name as a symbol of all that we have promised and all that we shall share.

11. The Declaration

The minister joins their right hands together and addresses the congregation

A and C have declared before God and before you that they will live together in Christian marriage; they have made sacred promises to each other, and have symbolized their marriage today by joining hands and by the giving and receiving of a ring/rings. I therefore pronounce them to be husband and wife, in the name of God, Father, Son, and Holy Spirit.

Whom God has joined together, let no one separate.

12. The Marriage Blessing

The couple may kneel

May the Lord bless you and take care of you;
may the Lord be kind and gracious to you;
may the Lord look on you with favour
and give you peace.
   Amen.

or

The Lord bless you and keep you;
the Lord make his face to shine upon you
and be gracious to you;
the Lord lift up his countenance upon you and
give you peace.
   Amen. *Num. 6: 24–6*

There may be added:

Blessed be God the Father
who gives joy to the bridegroom and bride:
Blessed be the Lord Jesus Christ
who brings new life to the world:
Blessed be the Holy Spirit of God
who brings us together in love.
Blessed be Father, Son, and Holy Spirit,
one God to be praised for ever.
   Amen.

13. Greetings

Husband and wife may embrace each other with a kiss. All may share the Peace together

14. Hymn

15. Scripture Reading(s) and Sermon

May be taken earlier

16. Prayers

Each grouping may conclude with a versicle and response, such as:
Lord hear us:
Lord, graciously hear us.

All grace comes from you, O God, and you alone
are the source of all love.
Bless your servants *A* and *C*,
that they may live together faithfully
to the end of their lives.

May they be gentle, patient, caring,
always ready to trust, help, and encourage each other,
to face together the challenge of the future.
Confirm them in their happiness,
that your joy may be in them,
and their joy may be full.
Strengthen them in their troubles, that they may
bear each other's burdens,
and so fulfil the law of Christ.
And give them grace when they hurt each other
to recognize and acknowledge their fault,
and ask each other's forgiveness and yours.

Bless their families and friends:
may they always thank you for them.

(Bless them in the gift of children:
may they be loving, wise, and caring parents.)

Let your peace dwell in their home:
may it be a sign of hope for others,
and a place of welcome:
may friend and stranger share its joy.
Loving one another in Christ,
may they be inspired to love Christ in their
neighbour.
Being creative in their daily work and leisure,
may they find fulfilment in the life of their
community.

Grant that we who have witnessed
the covenant of love sealed this day
may find our faith renewed,
our loyalties confirmed,
and our lives strengthened;
through Jesus Christ our Lord.
Amen.

The Lord's Prayer

The service may continue with the celebration of the Lord's Supper

17. Hymn

18. Blessing

May God, the source and giver of love,
fill you with all joy and peace,
that in Christ your love may be complete.
And the blessing of God almighty,
the Father, the Son, and the Holy Spirit,
be with you always.
Amen.

Scripture Readings

OLD TESTAMENT
Gen. 1: 26–8, 31a; 2: 18–25; Song of Solomon 8: 6–7a; Tobit 8: 5–9; Eccl. 26: 1–4;

NEW TESTAMENT
Rom. 12: 1–2, 9–13; 1 Cor. 13: 1–8a, 13; Eph. 3: 14–21; 5: 1–2, 25–33; Phil. 1: 9–11; Col. 3: 12–16a, 17; 1 John 3: 18–24; 4: 7–13; Matt. 7: 21, 24–7; Mark 10: 6–9; John 2: 1–11; 15: 9–12.

BLESSING OF A CIVIL MARRIAGE

1. The Welcome
2. Scripture Sentences
3. Prayer of Approach
4. Hymn
5. The Purpose of Marriage
6. Prayer of Assurance
7. The Promises
8. The Marriage Blessing
9. Greetings
10. Hymn
11. Scripture Reading(s) and Sermon
12. Prayers
13. Hymn
14. Blessing

The following service may be used after a Civil Marriage.

The Service of Blessing of a Civil Marriage in no way supersedes or invalidates any marriage previously solemnized, and record of it should not be entered in a marriage register.

1. The Welcome

The minister may greet and welcome the congregation, saying or concluding:

Grace to you and peace
from God our Father and the Lord Jesus Christ.

2. Scripture Sentences

Let us worship God.

O give thanks to the Lord, for he is good;
his steadfast love endures for ever. *Ps. 106: 1*

This is the day that the Lord has made;
let us rejoice and be glad in it. *Ps. 118: 24*

God created human beings in his own image;
in the image of God he created them;
male and female he created them. *Gen. 1: 27*

Many waters cannot quench love,
neither can floods drown it. *Song of Solomon 8: 7*

Dear friends, let us love one another,
because love is from God.
Everyone who loves is a child of God and knows God.
1 John 4: 7

[handwritten: WELCOME]

God is love, and those who live in love live in God,
and God lives in them. *1 John 4: 16 (adapted)*

[handwritten: HYMN   Lord of all hopefulness]

3. Prayer of Approach

O God, your gracious love surrounds us,
and everything we enjoy comes from you.
We confess our ingratitude for your goodness
and our selfishness in the use of your gifts.
We ask you to forgive us
and to fill us with your Spirit,
that we may worship you now with free and open hearts,
and serve you always with thankful and generous lives;
through Jesus Christ our Lord.
Amen.

4. Hymn

5. The Purpose of Marriage

We are gathered here in the presence of God to celebrate the marriage of *AB* and *CB* and to ask God's blessing on it.

Marriage is a gift and calling of God,
and is not to be entered upon lightly or thoughtlessly,
but reverently and responsibly,
in obedience to the gospel of Christ.

God has given us marriage so that husband and wife
may find comfort and companionship in each other,
and live faithfully together for the whole of their lives.

God has given us marriage so that husband and wife
may love and honour each other,
enrich and encourage each other,
and know each other with tenderness and joy.

God has given us marriage for the birth and nurture
of children, so that they may grow up in
the security of love, and come to experience
the freedom of faith.

God has given us marriage so that husband and wife,
being joined together as Christ with his Church,
may be a sign of unity and mutual commitment,
for the enrichment of society and the
strengthening of community.

6. Prayer for Assurance and Sincerity

God of love, ever-gracious and ever-kind,
we pray for *A* and *C* as they commit themselves to
Christian marriage.
In repentance and in faith may they know you
as a God of mercy and new beginnings,
who forgives our failures,
restores our wholeness,
and renews our hope.
God of love, ever-present and ever-faithful,
may *A* and *C* be conscious that their marriage
is both your will and your delight.
May the words they speak govern the life they
will lead.
May your presence surround them,
your faithfulness encourage them,
and your Spirit strengthen and guide them:
through Jesus Christ our Lord.
   Amen.

7. The Promises

The couple face each other and join their right hands

A, you have taken C to be your (lawful wedded) wife. Since you wish to acknowlege before God your desire that your married life should be according to his will, I therefore ask you:
will you love her, comfort her,
honour and protect her,
in times of prosperity and health,
and in times of trouble and suffering,
and be faithful to her
as long as you both shall live?
   I will.

C, you have taken A to be your (lawful wedded) husband. Since you wish to acknowledge before God your desire that your married life should be according to his will, I therefore ask you:
will you love him, comfort him,
honour and protect him,
in times of prosperity and health,
and in times of trouble and suffering,
and be faithful to him
as long as you both shall live?
   I will.

With his/her right hand on the couple's hands, the minister says:

May the ring(s) you wear be the symbol(s) of unending love, and reminder(s) of the promises made this day.

May you love and cherish each other till death parts you.

Whom God has joined together, let no one separate.

8. The Marriage Blessing

The couple may kneel

May the Lord bless you and take care of you;
may the Lord be kind and gracious to you;
may the Lord look on you with favour
and give you peace.
   Amen.

BLESSING OF A CIVIL MARRIAGE

or

The Lord bless you and keep you;
the Lord make his face to shine on you and be gracious to you;
the Lord lift up his countenance on you and give you peace.
   Amen   *Num. 6: 24–6*

There may be added:

Blessed be God the Father
who gives joy to the bridegroom and bride;
Blessed be the Lord Jesus Christ
who brings new life to the world:
Blessed be the Holy Spirit of God
who brings us together in love.
Blessed be Father, Son, and Holy Spirit,
one God to be praised for ever.
   Amen.

9. Greetings

Husband and wife may embrace each other with a kiss. They and the congregation may also share the Peace

10. Hymn

11. Scripture Reading(s) and Sermon

12. Prayers

The service may continue with prayers for the couple, for Christian family life, for the gift of children, and for concerns outside the family, concluding with the Lord's Prayer, as in the Wedding Service. The service may continue with the celebration of the Lord's Supper.

13. Hymn

14. Blessing

May God, the source and giver of love,
fill you with all joy and peace,
that in Christ your love may be complete.
And the blessing of God almighty,
the Father, the Son, and the Holy Spirit,
be with you always.
Amen.

See the Wedding Service appendix for readings.

THE FUNERAL

A Service of Witness to the Resurrection

1. Scripture Sentences
2. Preface
3. Hymn
4. Prayers
5. Scripture Readings
6. Sermon
7. Hymn
8. Prayers of Confident Faith
9. The Committal
10. Prayers
11. Dismissal and Blessing

1. Scripture Sentences

I am the resurrection and the life, says the Lord. Those who have faith in me shall live, even though they die; and no one who lives and has faith in me shall ever die.   *John 11: 25–6 (adapted)*

The eternal God is your dwelling-place, and underneath are the everlasting arms.   *Deut. 33: 27*

Cast your burden on the Lord, and he will sustain you.
Ps. 55: 22

God is our refuge and strength, a very present help in trouble.
Ps. 46: 1

In God's favour is life; weeping may endure for a night, but joy comes in the morning.   *Ps. 30: 5*

Blessed are those who mourn, for they shall be comforted.
Matt. 5: 4

God so loved the world that he gave his only Son, that everyone who has faith in him should not perish but have eternal life.
John 3: 16

I am convinced that there is nothing in death or life, in the realm of spirits or superhuman powers, in the world as it is or the world as it shall be, in the forces of the universe, in heights, or depths—nothing in all creation that can separate us from the love of God in Christ Jesus our Lord. *Rom. 8: 38–9*

Praise be to the God and Father of our Lord Jesus Christ, the all-merciful Father, the God whose consolation never fails us! He comforts us in all our troubles, so that we in turn may be able to comfort others in any trouble of theirs and to share with them the consolation we ourselves receive from God. *2 Cor. 1: 3–4*

As a father has compassion on his children, so the Lord has compassion on those that fear him. *Ps. 103: 13*

As a mother comforts her child so I will comfort you, says the Lord. *Isa. 66: 13*

He shall feed his flock like a shepherd. He will gather the lambs in his arms and he will carry them in his bosom.

Isa. 40: 11

Praise be to the God and Father of our Lord Jesus Christ, who in his great mercy gave us new birth into a living hope by the resurrection of Jesus Christ from the dead!

1 Pet. 1: 3

2. Preface

We have come together to worship God and to give thanks and praise for the life of *AB* . . . We have come to pray for the comfort and strength that God promises to us. We have come to affirm the Christian conviction that death is not the end—but a new beginning.

Jesus says: 'Those who come to me I will not cast out.'

or

We have come together to worship God; to give thanks and praise for the life of *AB* . . ., whose days among us have now drawn to a close. We have come to share our grief over one loved and respected by those who knew *her/him*, and one whose love and concern have strengthened us.

THE FUNERAL

We meet in the faith that death is not the ultimate calamity that it seems; that we can be enabled to face it despite fear, anger, bitterness, or guilt.

3. Hymn

4. Prayers

God who gave us birth, you are ever more ready to hear than we are to pray. You know our needs before we ask, and our ignorance in asking. Show us now your grace, that as we face the mystery of death we may see the light of eternity. Speak to us once more your joyful message of life and of death overcome. Help us to live as those who are prepared to die, and when our days here are ended, enable us to die as those who go forth and live, so that living or dying our life may be in Jesus Christ our risen saviour.
Amen.

or

God our Father, our refuge and strength, a helper close at hand in time of trouble: you can change the shadow of death into the brightness of a new morning. We turn to you now, and to your Word, so that we may renew our trust and our hope, and be lifted from darkness and distress into the light and peace of your presence; through Jesus Christ our Lord.
Amen.

or

Gracious God, enable us to listen lovingly for your Word. May we console each other with the message you proclaim, so finding light in darkness and faith in the midst of doubt; through Jesus Christ our Lord.
Amen.

or

God of life and love, we come to you in our need. Be with us as we experience the abyss of death and grief. Be there in our sorrow and pain; be with us in our fear, that we may find light in darkness, comfort in your Word; in the name of Jesus, who by death has conquered death.

Amen.

THE MINISTRY OF THE WORD

5. Scripture Readings (Readings from the Old Testament and Psalms are listed on page 74).

> The Spirit of God affirms to our spirit that we are God's children; and if children, then heirs, heirs of God and fellow-heirs with Christ; but we must share his sufferings if we are also to share his glory.
>
> For I reckon that the sufferings we now endure bear no comparison with the glory, as yet unrevealed, which is in store for us.
>
> In everything, as we know, he co-operates for good with those who love God and are called according to his purpose.
>
> With all this in mind, what are we to say? If God is on our side, who is against us? He did not spare his own Son, but gave him up for us all; how can he fail to lavish every other gift upon us? Who will bring a charge against those whom God has chosen? Not God, who acquits! Who will pronounce judgement? Not Christ, who died, or rather rose again; not Christ, who is at God's right hand and pleads our cause! Then what can separate us from the love of Christ? Can affliction or hardship? Can persecution, hunger, nakedness, danger, or sword? ('We are being done to death for your sake, all day long' as Scripture says: 'We have been treated like sheep for slaughter') and yet, throughout it all, overwhelming victory is ours through him who loved us. For I am convinced that there is nothing in death or life, in the realm of spirits or superhuman powers, in the world as it is or the world as it shall be, in the forces of the universe, in heights or depths—nothing in all creation that can separate us from the love of God in Jesus Christ our Lord.
>
> Rom. 8: 16–18, 28, 31–5, 37–9

THE FUNERAL

I may speak in tongues of men or of angels,
but if I have no love, I am a sounding gong or a
  clanging cymbal.
I may have the gift of prophecy and the knowledge
  of every hidden truth;
I may have faith enough to move mountains;
but if I have no love, I am nothing.
I may give all I possess to the needy,
I may give my body to be burnt,
but if I have no love, I gain nothing by it.
Love is patient and kind.
Love envies no one, is never boastful, never conceited,
never rude; love is never selfish, never quick to take
  offence.
Love keeps no score of wrongs, takes no pleasure
in the sins of others, but delights in the truth.
There is nothing love cannot face;
there is no limit to its faith, its hope, its endurance.
Love will never come to an end.
Prophecies will cease; tongues of ecstasy will fall silent;
  knowledge will vanish.
For our knowledge and our prophecy alike are partial,
and the partial vanishes when wholeness comes.
When I was a child I spoke like a child,
thought like a child, reasoned like a child;
but when I grew up I finished with childish things.
At present we see only puzzling reflections in a mirror,
but one day we shall see face to face.
My knowledge now is partial;
then it will be whole, like God's knowledge of me.
There are three things that last for ever:
faith, hope, and love;
and the greatest of the three is love. *1 Cor. 13: 1–13*

If it is for this life only that Christ has given us hope, we of all people are most to be pitied.

But the truth is, Christ was raised to life—the first-fruits of the harvest of the dead. For since it was a man who brought death into the world, a man also brought resurrection of the dead. As in Adam all die, so in Christ all will be brought to life; but each in proper order: Christ the first-fruits, and afterwards at his coming, those who belong to Christ. Then comes the end, when he delivers up the kingdom to God the Father, after deposing every sovereignty, authority, and power. For he is destined to reign until God has put all enemies under his feet; and the last enemy to be deposed is death.

But, you may ask, how are the dead raised? In what kind of body? What stupid questions! The seed you sow does not come to life unless it has first died; and what you sow is not the body that shall be, but a bare grain, of wheat perhaps, or something else; and God gives it the body of his choice, each seed its own particular body.

So it is with the resurrection of the dead: what is sown as a perishable thing is raised imperishable. Sown in humiliation, it is raised in glory; sown in weakness, it is raised in power; sown a physical body, it is raised a spiritual body.

What I mean, my friends, is this: flesh and blood can never possess the kingdom of God, the perishable cannot possess the imperishable.

(Listen! I will unfold a mystery: we shall not all die, but we shall all be changed in a flash, in the twinkling of an eye, at the last trumpet-call. For the trumpet will sound, and the dead will rise imperishable, and we shall be changed.)

This perishable body must be clothed with the imperishable, and what is mortal with immortality. And when this perishable body has been clothed with the imperishable and our mortality has been clothed with immortality, then the saying of scripture will come true: 'Death is swallowed up; victory is won!' 'O Death, where is your victory? O Death, where is your sting?' The sting of death is sin, and sin gains its power from the law. But thanks be to God! He gives us victory through our Lord Jesus Christ.

Therefore, my dear friends, stand firm and immovable, and work for the Lord always, work without limit, since you know that in the Lord your labour cannot be lost.

I Cor. 15: 19–26, 35–8, 42–4, 50–8

THE FUNERAL

I saw a new heaven and a new earth, for the first heaven and the first earth had vanished, and there was no longer any sea. I saw the Holy City, new Jerusalem, coming down out of heaven from God, made ready like a bride adorned for her husband. I heard a loud voice proclaiming from the throne: 'Now God has his dwelling with mankind! He will dwell among them and they shall be his people, and God himself will be with them. He will wipe every tear from their eyes. There shall be an end to death, and to mourning and crying and pain, for the old order has passed away!'

The One who sat on the throne said: 'I am making all things new!' ('Write this down,' he said: 'for these words are trustworthy and true.') Then he said to me: 'It is done! I am the Alpha and the Omega, the beginning and the end. To the thirsty I will give water from the spring of life as a gift. This is the victors' heritage; and I will be their God and they will be my children.'

Rev. 21: 1–7

Then the angel showed me the river of the water of life, sparkling like a crystal, flowing from the throne of God and of the Lamb down the middle of the city's street. On either side of the river stood a tree of life, which yields twelve crops of fruit, one for each month of the year. The leaves of the trees are for the healing of the nations. Every accursed thing shall disappear. The throne of God and the Lamb will be there, and his servants shall worship him; they shall see him face to face and bear his name on their foreheads. There shall be no more night, nor will they need the light of lamp or sun, for the Lord God will give them light; and they shall reign for ever.

Rev. 22: 1–5

'Set your troubled hearts at rest. Trust in God always; trust also in me. There are many dwelling-places in my Father's house; if it were not so I should have told you; for I am going to prepare a place for you. And if I go and prepare a place for you, I shall come again and take you to myself, so that where I am you may be also; and you know the way I am taking.' Thomas said: 'Lord, we do not know where you are going, so how can we know the way?' Jesus replied: 'I am the way, the truth, and the life; no one comes to the Father except by me.'

'I will not leave you bereft; I am coming back to you. In a little while the world will see me no longer, but you will see me; because I live, you too will live.'

'Peace is my parting gift to you, my own peace, such as the world cannot give. Set your troubled hearts at rest, and banish your fears.'
John 14: 1–6, 18–19, 27

Further Readings:

PSALMS

Pss. 23; 103: 8–18; 123; 121; 90: 1–6, 10, 12; 139: 13–18.

OLD TESTAMENT

Isa. 25: 6–9; 26: 3–4; 61: 1–3; 40: 6–10, 28–31; 11: 6–9. Lam. 3: 17–26, 31–3; Job. 19: 1, 23–7b.

NEW TESTAMENT

1 John 3: 1–2; John 6: 37–40; 5: 19–24; 11: 17–27

6. Sermon on the Christian Hope

7. Hymn of Confident Faith

8. Prayers

Thanksgiving for the Victory of Christ

Gracious God, whose purpose for all people is one of good, from whose love nothing can separate us, neither death nor life, nor things present nor things to come, we offer you our thanks and praise for all that you have done for the human family through Jesus Christ. By giving him to live and die for us, you have made known your ways with men and women, and shown that your love has no limit. By raising him from the dead, you have promised that those who trust in him will share his resurrection-life. Grant us, then, that confidence in you, which, even in the hour of deep distress and great perplexity, clings to your guiding hand and finds strength and comfort; through Jesus Christ our Lord.
Amen.

or

God, our Father, we thank you that you sent your Son Jesus Christ to die for us and rise again. His cross declares your love to be without limit; his resurrection, that death our last enemy, is doomed. By his victory we are assured of the promise that you will never leave us or forsake us; that neither death nor life, nor things present nor things to come, can separate us from your love in Christ Jesus our Lord.

Amen.

Commendation of the Departed

Eternal God, before whose face the generations rise and pass away: we praise you for all your servants departed this life in your faith and love, especially for *A* . . ., whom today we commend into your sure keeping; each of us recalling in a moment of silence what *she/he* has meant to *her/his* loved ones, friends, and colleagues. We give thanks for all your goodness to *her/him*; all *she/he* accomplished by your grace; and all that *she/he* was to those who loved *her/him*. And now we praise you that for *her/him* sorrow and sickness are ended, death itself is past, and *she/he* lives for ever in your love and care; through Jesus Christ our Lord.

Amen.

Petition

O God, who brought us to birth, and in whose arms we die, in our grief and shock, contain and comfort us; embrace us with your love, give us hope in our confusion, and grace to let go into new life; through Jesus Christ.

Amen.

or

Almighty God, we pray that, encouraged by the example of your saints, we may run with patience the race that is set before us, looking to Jesus, the pioneer and perfecter of our faith; so that at the last we may join those whom we love in your presence where there is fullness of joy; through Jesus Christ our Lord.

Amen.

Thanksgiving, Commendation, and Petition

Let us approach our loving Creator with thanksgiving. Let us give thanks, even in our distress, for the promise and hope which God has given us in Jesus, who lived and died and lives again.

or

Let us give thanks for those who have died in the faith, who live and surround us, a great cloud of witnesses, with whom we lift up our hearts to God.

Silence

Let us be thankful especially for the life and love of *A* . . ., whom we commit to your care, each of us recalling in silence what *she/he* meant to us.

Help us to believe that death is the gateway to a fuller life and that *she/he* is safe in your keeping.

Silence

God of all consolation, in your unending love and mercy you turn the darkness of death into the dawn of a new life. Show compassion to your people in their sorrow. Be our refuge and our strength, to lift us from the darkness of grief to the peace and light of your presence. Your Son, our Lord Jesus Christ, by dying for us conquered death, and by rising again restored life. May we then go forward eagerly to meet him and after our life on earth be reunited with our loved ones where every tear will be wiped away. We ask this through Jesus Christ, sustainer and redeemer.

Commendation, Petition, and Intercession

Intimate God,
you are able to accept in us
what we cannot even acknowledge;
you have named in us
what we cannot bear to speak of;
you hold in your memory
what we have tried to forget;
you will hold out to us
a glory we cannot imagine.

THE FUNERAL

Reconcile us through your cross
to all that we have rejected in ourselves,
that we may find no part of your creation
to be alien or strange to us,
and that we ourselves may be made whole,
> through Jesus Christ, our lover and our friend,
> **Amen.**

Silence

Help us confess any hurt, and wrong we feel we have done to
A . . ., and help us to know that we are forgiven, even as we hear
your words: 'Those who come to me, I will not cast out.'

Silence

Living, loving God, give us joy deeper than sorrow as we thank
you for all your children and especially for *A* . . ., whom we now
commit into your care and keeping.

As *she/he* was sustained and fed at your table on earth, welcome
her/him at the banquet of your children in heaven.

We give thanks that for *A* . . ., pain and sorrow are ended, that
death itself is past, and that *she/he* lives for ever in your love and
care.

Silence

And since we have all been but a hair's breadth from death since
birth, teach us, O God, how close we are to that life in all its
fullness which Christ alone can give.

Let us be thankful that Jesus has sent his Spirit to wipe away all
tears from our eyes, to bind up our wounded spirits, to give us
peace in the midst of our trouble, for he is with us now and
always.

Silence

Let us pray for . . . (*members of the bereaved family are named*) and
all whom they love. For them we ask for resources stronger than
anything we can offer: peace, joy, and hope; gifts that no one, no
grief, can take away. May they grieve, but not as those without
hope.

Silence

Sustaining and all-loving God, we pray also for others around the world who bear pain and grief, guilt and fear. May they find the peace and the wholeness, the healing and the joy we seek.

We pray through Jesus Christ your Son, our Lord, who died and rose again to save us, and is now alive and reigns with you and the Holy Spirit in glory for ever.
   Amen.

The Lord's Prayer

Ascription of glory

(Where the committal is to be in another place this part of the service may end with a hymn and an ascription of glory such as:

Now to the One who can keep you from falling
and set you in the presence of his glory,
jubilant and above reproach,
to the only God our Saviour,
be glory and majesty, might and authority,
through Jesus Christ our Lord,
before all time, now and evermore.   *Jude 24, 25*
   Amen.)

9. The Committal

Jesus says: 'I am the resurrection and the life. Those who have faith in me shall live, even though they die; and no one who lives and has faith in me shall ever die.'   *John 11: 25 (adapted)*

If we live, we live for the Lord; and if we die, we die for the Lord. So whether we live or die, we belong to the Lord.
                                       Rom. 14: 8

The Lord says: 'Do not be afraid. I am the first and the last, and I am the living One; I was dead and now I am alive for evermore, and I hold the keys of death and death's domain.
                              Rev. 1: 17–18 (adapted)

THE FUNERAL

In sure and certain hope of the resurrection to eternal life, through our Lord Jesus Christ, we commend to almighty God our *sister/brother* A . . . and commit *her/his* mortal body to the elements / *to the ground: earth to earth*, ashes to ashes, dust to dust, trusting in the infinite mercy of God and the victory of Christ our Lord.

Amen.

or

Having commended into God's hands A . . ., we commit *her/his* body to the ground / *to be cremated: earth to earth*, ashes to ashes, dust to dust, putting our whole trust and confidence in the mercy of our heavenly Father, and in the victory of his Son, Jesus Christ our Lord, who died, and was buried and rose again for us, and lives and reigns forever.

Amen.

or

Now that the earthly life of A . . . has come to an end, we commit *her/his* body to be *buried/cremated* confident of the resurrection to eternal life, through our Lord Jesus Christ.

Amen.

He will wipe away every tear from their eyes, and death shall be no more, neither shall there be mourning or crying nor pain anymore, for the former things have passed away.

Rev. 21: 4

They shall never again feel hunger or thirst, the sun shall not beat on them nor any scorching heat, because the Lamb who is at the heart of the throne will be their shepherd and will guide them to the springs of the water of life; and God will wipe away all tears from their eyes.   *Rev. 7: 16–17*

Te Deum

You, Christ, are the king of glory,
the eternal Son of the Father.
When you took our flesh to set us free
you humbly chose the Virgin's womb.

You overcame the sting of death
and opened the kingdom of heaven to all believers.
You are seated at God's right hand in glory.
We believe that you will come to be our judge.
> Come then, Lord, and help your people,
> bought with the price of your own blood,
> and bring us with your saints
> to glory everylasting.

10. Prayers

Almighty God, you have bound together all your people in heaven and on earth in one holy fellowship: let not our thoughts linger here, but help us to believe that your servant's life has made a new beginning, with your mercy and your love still around *her/him*. Strengthened by this assurance, may we return to the duties which await us in the world, resolved to be more faithful to you and more helpful to one another, for the sake of those no longer with us upon earth; through Jesus Christ our Lord.
Amen.

or

Lord, support us by your grace through all the hours of life's day: until the shadows lengthen, the busy world is hushed, the fever of life is over, and the evening comes. Then Lord, in your mercy, grant us a safe lodging, a holy rest, and peace at the last; through Jesus Christ our Lord.
Amen.

11. Dismissal and Blessing

The peace of God, which passes all understanding, keep your hearts and minds in the knowledge and love of God and of his Son, Jesus Christ our Lord. And the blessing of God almighty, the Father, the Son, and the Holy Spirit, be among you, and remain with you always.
Amen

THE FUNERAL
APPENDIX

Additional Prayers for use at Funerals

At the Funeral of a Child

Lord, your knowledge of us is perfect for you have made us and you love us through and through. Our knowledge of you is partial and incomplete.

Help us then to trust what you have shown us of your love for us, to know that what you have begun in Christ you will complete.

Bring us with *A* . . . to know you as fully as you know us, to see you face to face through Jesus Christ our Lord.
Amen.

Lord, we find not only death but love itself painful because *A* . . . whom we love has died.

We come to you now because we believe that you share our grief. Help us to trust you and find comfort in you as we give thanks for *A* . . .'s life.

We thank you for all that *she/he* has meant to us, for the times *she/he* has made us laugh, and the times *she/he* made us cry, for the love shared together because of *her/him*.

Forgive us for any ways in which we may have failed *her/him* and help us to accept that we are forgiven.

Help us to trust that *she/he* continues in your love and care, that in your keeping *she/he* is whole and safe. Be with those whose lives have been most closely knit with *A* . . .'s, especially . . . Help us through *A* . . .'s death to see more deeply into the meaning of *her/his* life and of our own, to grasp more firmly that life is not to be valued according to its length, that love is stronger than death.

As we give thanks for *A* . . ., we commit ourselves to live for you and one another, relying on your help. Lord, give us all we need for our journey; give us hope and peace. Be with us here and everywhere; be present with us now and always, fulfiller of our past, strength of our present, and promise of our future; through Jesus Christ our Lord.
Amen.

At The Funeral of a Still-Born Child

Lord, you love us from all eternity and from the moment when you shaped and formed us in our mother's womb. We give thanks for *A* . . ., for the wonder of *her/his* being, so closely knit with ours. Lord, you know *A* . . . through and through and you love *her/him* for you created *her/his* innermost self. Help us now as we entrust *A* . . . to you knowing that *she/he* is safe in your care.

Be close to these parents in their grief. May *A* . . . bring them new understanding and a deepening love for one another. May we know ourselves to be enfolded in your love until with *A* . . . and all your children we are gathered into one through Jesus Christ our Lord.
Amen.

For Use in Particularly Distressing Circumstances

Lord, we join together today in thanking you for *A* . . ., we thank you for *her/him* as a person, for all *her/his* qualities, for all that *she/he* was able to give and receive during *her/his* life.

We entrust *her/him* into your hands knowing that you alone are the one who is able to satisfy all the longings of *her/his* heart.

Lord, you are the one who brings good out of evil; out of death you brought resurrection. You are the one who can bring something new out of *A* . . .'s tragic death.

We pray for all of us who have been touched by *A* . . .'s life and death. Help us to hear what you are saying to us. Turn us away from all that we know to be wrong; help us to show love and understanding to those around us.

Forgive us for any ways in which we may have hurt *A* . . ., help us to know that you are always ready to forgive us and to offer us a new beginning when we turn to you. Keep us in your grace, guide and protect us, until with *A* . . . and all your children we find ourselves truly at home in your great love; through Jesus Christ, our Lord,
Amen.

Prayer at The Burial or Scattering of Ashes

Scripture sentences

We remember *A* . . . with gratitude and affection, and give thanks for *her/him*. We say again that this is not the end, for our God is the God who raised Jesus from the dead and will bring us all to life. In this faith we now commit *her/his* ashes *to the ground* (to their final resting place).

Lord, we remember your love toward us and all your people, and especially we remember your love for your *daughter/son A* . . .

We give you thanks that your love never comes to an end, that whether we live or die we belong to you.

We give you thanks for all that *A* . . . still means to us, and we pray for ourselves, that we may continue to grow in love until we reach the full stature of Christ, in whom all things are one; we ask it in his name.
Amen.

The Blessing

ORDINATION AND INDUCTION OF MINISTERS

1. Scripture Sentences
2. Prayers
3. Scripture Readings
4. Sermon (This may be taken after the Right Hand of Fellowship)
5. Statements
6. The Affirmations
7. The Ordination/Induction
8. Declaration
9. Presentation
10. Right Hand of Fellowship
11. Prayers of Intercession
12. Dismissal and Blessing

A service of ordination to the Ministry of the Word and Sacraments and of induction to a pastorate is held under the authority of a District Council. The Moderator of the Synod is invited by the Council to preside. The service is normally held in the pastorate to which the minister is inducted.

APPROACH TO GOD

1. Scripture Sentences

You are Christ's body. Christ is head of his body, the Church. He is the source of its life; he was raised from death over all things supreme.

Through him God chose to reconcile all things to himself.

Jesus Christ is Lord.

Let us exalt his name for ever.

In Christ we have boldness and confidence of access through our faith in him.

Give thanks to him and bless his name.

2. Prayers

Prayers of adoration and confession such as the following may be used.

We praise and adore you, God, the creator: through your love and power all things came to be, and continue in their being.

We praise and adore you, Jesus Christ, the Word made flesh: through your death on the cross we are reconciled to the Father, and by your rising we are born again into a living hope.

We praise and adore you, Holy Spirit, the Giver of life: through your fire the Church was born, and by your gifts the body of Christ is built up.

With the whole Church on earth and in heaven we praise and adore you, Father, Son, and Holy Spirit, one God, for ever.

Let us confess our sin:

Gracious God, why are we called the body of Christ?
We are not worthy of his name.
Christ proclaimed truth—we obscure it.
Christ prayed for the unity of all—we are divided.
Christ opened the way to your presence—we have shut people out.
We shrink from the demands of justice—Christ touched the sick and blessed the poor.
We love our friends—Christ loved his enemies.
We hide in the Church—Christ gave himself for the world.
Forgive us.
Conform us to Christ.
May all that we do arise from our unity with him.
May his life renew the life of the world.
In the name of Christ. Amen.

In repentance and in faith hear the promise of grace and the assurance of pardon. Here are words you may trust, words that merit full acceptance: 'Christ Jesus came into the world to save sinners.' 'Your sins are forgiven.' To all who turn to him he says, 'Follow me'.

Thanks be to God.

God of life and power,
we open our hearts and rejoice
that the depth of your being is love.
We praise you for showing us in Jesus
what you call us to be.
Come in the power of your Spirit
to bring us together and make us your own
to the glory of Christ our Lord.
Amen.

The presiding minister explains that the ordination and/or induction service is a meeting of the District Council as well as of the local church or group of churches. Representatives of civic bodies and other churches may be welcomed. Mention should be made of a candidate's call to the ministry having been recognized by the church and training for it completed satisfactorily. The remarks conclude as follows:

In the name of the Lord Jesus Christ, the head of the Church, we come

in the case of ordination to ordain *AB* to the ministry of the Word and Sacraments and to serve as minister, *as chaplain, auxiliary minister, etc.* in *YZ*.	**in the case of induction only** to induct *AB* to serve as minister, *as chaplain, auxiliary minister, etc.* in *YZ*.

MINISTRY OF THE WORD

Let us listen for the Word of God in the Scriptures.

3. Scripture Readings

See the readings appended to this service.

4. Sermon *(This may be taken later)*

ACT OF ORDINATION AND INDUCTION

5. Statements

A statement may be made relating briefly the circumstances leading to the call.

The minister-elect may make a statment about his/her *faith and sense of calling.*

A statement concerning the Nature, Faith, and Order of the United Reformed Church (Schedule D) is read in one of the approved forms.

6. The Affirmations

The minister-elect makes his/her *affirmations (Schedule C in 'The Manual'). The questions may require some modification for ministry in other spheres. The words of the ordination/induction prayer will also need adapting.*

The congregation is invited to stand to re-affirm their faith and make their promises.

Do you confess again your faith in one God, Father, Son, and Holy Spirit?
   We do.

Do you receive *AB* . . ., as from God, to serve among you here and with you in the world?
   We do.

Will you pray for *him/her* and for each other, seeking together the will of God, and will you give *him/her* due honour, consideration, and encouragement, building one another up in faith, hope, and love?

   We will, by the grace of God.

The members of the District Council present are addressed.

Do you welcome *AB* . . . into membership of the District Council, promising to sustain *him/her* in *his/her* service?
   We do.

ORDINATION AND INDUCTION OF MINISTERS 89

A hymn or anthem may be sung as a prayer for the blessing of the Spirit; it may be sung seated.

7. The Ordination/Induction

The congregation is invited to stand; the ordinand kneels; a minister only being inducted need not do so.

Lord God, we offer you praise and thanksgiving.
Out of love for the world you sent Jesus Christ,
who humbled himself, became a servant, suffered and died on a cross.
You glorified him, raising him from the dead.
We glorify his name above all other names.
Now we pray for his love and humility in all our service.
We praise and thank you too for creating the Church and blessing her with the gifts of your Spirit; and we remember with gratitude all your servants who have witnessed faithfully to the Gospel of Christ.

For ordination

And now we thank you especially for calling *AB* to serve you as a minister in your Church.

Those appointed by the District Council lay their hands on the ordinand's head.

For induction only

Today we thank you in particular for the service that *AB* has given in *XY* and we pray that *his/her* sense of your calling may be renewed as *he/she* comes to this work.

FILL YOUR SERVANT *AB* . . . WITH YOUR HOLY SPIRIT, AS IN YOUR NAME AND IN OBEDIENCE TO YOUR WILL WE ORDAIN *HIM/HER* TO BE A MINISTER IN YOUR CHURCH.

The President, Interim Moderator, or another may continue in their own words or as follows:

Gracious God, dwell with *A* . . . and strengthen the gifts you have given *him/her* that the ministry and mission of your people may bear fruit.

Inspire *him/her* in leading worship, in preaching and teaching and service; may the gospel be celebrated when *he/she* presides at the Sacraments.

Bless *him/her* with love and humility to tend your flock, to feed the hungry, heal the wounded, and find the lost.

Give *him/her* power and patience to witness with all Christians to your way, and to labour with all people of good will for justice and mercy in society.

Watch over *him/her* in times of trial: in weariness, disappointment, or frustration; and keep *him/her* from complacency and spiritual pride.

Fill *his/her* home with your peace. *(Here special prayers may be made for members of the minister's household.)*

Give grace to the people of *this church/these churches* that they may accept the service God offers them through *AB*. May they work together for the glory of your name.

This we pray through Jesus Christ, who lives and reigns with you, Father, and the Holy Spirit, one God, for ever.
   Amen.

8. Declaration

Ordination and Induction

Representing the . . . District Council acting on behalf of the United Reformed Church in the United Kingdom, in the name of the Lord Jesus Christ I now declare *A* . . . to be ordained to the ministry of the Word and Sacraments in the Church of Jesus Christ, and to be inducted to the pastorate of *this/these* congregation(s) *(chaplaincy, etc.)*.

Induction

Representing the . . . District Council, acting on behalf of the United Reformed Church in the United Kingdom, in the name of the Lord Jesus Christ I declare *A* . . . to be inducted to the pastorate of *this/these* congregation(s) *(chaplaincy, etc.)*.

May the God of peace, who brought from the dead our Lord Jesus, the great shepherd of the sheep, by the blood of the eternal covenant, make you perfect in all goodness, so that you may do his will; and may he make us what he would have us be; through Jesus Christ, to whom be the glory for ever and ever.
Amen.

9. Presentation

A Bible may be presented to the minister with words such as:

We present you with this Bible. Here are the words of eternal life. Build up God's people in his truth, and serve them in his name.

10. Right Hand of Fellowship

The right hand of fellowship is given by the presiding minister and others duly appointed

The sermon may be preached here

11. Prayers of Intercession and The Lord's Prayer

It is suggested that the Interim Moderator may lead these prayers

An offering may be taken

The Lord's Supper may follow

12. Dismissal and Blessing

Scripture Readings

OLD TESTAMENT

Exod. 33: 12–14; Deut. 30: 11–20; 1 Kings 19: 1–21; Neh. 8: 1–12; Isa. 6: 1–8; 49: 1–6; 52: 7–10; 55: 1–13; 61: 1–4.

NEW TESTAMENT

It is recommended that one reading should come from the Gospels.

Acts 20: 17–38; Rom. 10: 5–15; 12: 1–21; 1 Cor. 12: 4–13; 2 Cor. 4: 1–15; Eph. 3: 8–21; 4: 1–16; Phil. 2: 1–16; 1 Pet. 4: 8–11; 5: 1–4; Matt. 5: 1–12; Mark 3: 13–19; 6:30–44; 10: 35–45; Luke 4: 14–21; 10: 1–11; John 13: 1–17; 15: 1–17.

COMMISSIONING OF CHURCH-RELATED COMMUNITY WORKERS

The Commissioning of a Church-Related Community Worker takes place at a service conducted by the District Council (where possible in one of the churches within the local community where he/she is to work). Representatives of civic bodies and other churches may be welcomed. The District Chairman constitutes the District Council in the presence of the congregation and then invites the Provincial Moderator to preside.

The Order of Worship may follow that to which the particular church is accustomed. It should begin with a Call to Worship and include Scripture Reading(s), Prayer(s), Hymn(s), and Sermon or Charge; and it may include Communion.

1. Preface
2. Statement and Affirmations
3. The Commissioning Prayer
4. Declaration
5. Right Hand of Fellowship
6. The Blessing

1. Preface

The Lord Jesus Christ continues his ministry to the world in and through the Church, the whole people of God called and committed to his service.

To equip them for this ministry, he gives particular gifts for particular ministries and calls some of his servants to exercise them in offices duly recognized within his Church.

Among the offices so recognized by the United Reformed Church is that of Church-Related Community Worker. A Church-Related Community Worker is a church member who has been accepted, trained, and appointed to an approved post within the church, to enable the church to work with the community.

AB has been appointed Community Worker with . . . church(es) and we meet, therefore, representing the . . . District Council and in association with the elders and members of *this/these* local church(es) to commission *him/her* to this office, praying for *him/her* as *he/she* dedicates *himself/herself* to this task. Let us recall the Nature, Faith, and Order of the United Reformed Church as set out in the *Basis of Union*.

2. Statement and Affirmations

A Statement concerning the Nature, Faith, and Order of the URC (Schedule D) is read in one of the approved forms.

The Community Worker stands and makes his/her affirmations:

AB we ask you now to reaffirm your faith and dedicate yourself to this new responsibility.

Do you confess anew your faith in one God, Father, Son, and Holy Spirit?
   I do.

In dependence on God's grace do you reaffirm your trust in Jesus Christ as Saviour and Lord and your promise to follow him and to seek to do and to bear his will all the days of your life?
   I do.

Do you believe that the Word of God in the Old and New Testaments, discerned under the guidance of the Holy Spirit, is the supreme authority for the faith and conduct of all God's people?
   I do.

Do you promise to care and to pray for the community, to give guidance to others as you yourself receive guidance from God, and to mediate the love and mercy of God to all those whom he gives to you as neighbours?
   I do.

Do you promise to share in building up the Church so that it can play its part in co-operation with others in fulfilling God's purpose in the world?
   I do.

COMMISSIONING OF COMMUNITY WORKERS

Do you undertake to exercise your ministry in accordance with the Nature, Faith, and Order of the United Reformed Church, and as opportunity arises to share in ministry with workers from this and other branches of the Church?

I do.

All now stand, and the members of the local church(es), and the representatives of the District Council answer the following questions:

Do you recognize the calling of *AB* to be a Church-Related Community Worker, and do you receive *him/her* to serve with you?

We do.

Do you promise to pray for each other, and for *AB*, to share with *him/her* in seeking and doing the will of God, to give *him/her* encouragement, consideration, and support, building *him/her* up in faith, hope, and love?

We do.

3. The Commissioning Prayer

The Community Worker may kneel and all others are invited to remain standing for the prayer of commissioning, which is offered in this or some other suitable form:

Most merciful God, you have set your Church in the world to bear witness to the gospel, and you equip it with the gifts it needs. We thank you that now, in this place, you have given us living proof of the way you call people into new realms of service.

Accept *AB* as now, in response to your call, *he/she* offers *himself/herself* (anew) for your service. Enrich *him/her* with the Holy Spirit and give *him/her* grace to be faithful in *his/her* work. Lead *him/her* into an ever deeper understanding of you and your kingdom, and sustain *his/her* sense of calling. Through *his/her* daily encounter with other people may they find their full humanity, be reconciled to yourself, and be made new in Christ, in his name we pray.

Amen.

4. Declaration

In the name of the Lord Jesus Christ the only head of the Church and in accordance with the decision of the District Council I declare you to be a Church-Related Community Worker commissioned by the United Reformed Church and appointed to work with the . . . (local church(es)) and the . . . District.

5. The Right Hand of Fellowship

In token of which I give you the right hand of fellowship.

The right hand of fellowship may also be given by representatives of the local church(es), the District Council, and the General Assembly.

The Service may continue with prayers, communion, and hymns, and conclude with:

6. The Blessing

Scripture Readings

OLD TESTAMENT

Isa. 42: 1–7; 49: 1–6; 61: 1–4

NEW TESTAMENT

John 13: 1–17; Rom. 1: 8–17; 12: 1–21; Matt. 11: 2–6; Eph. 4: 1–13; Luke 6: 31–8

ORDINATION AND INDUCTION OF ELDERS

1. Introduction
2. The Affirmations
3. The Ordination
4. The Induction

The ordination and induction of elders takes place when the local church meets for a service of the Word and Sacrament. The minister or interim moderator presides.

1. Introduction

The Lord Jesus continues his ministry in and through the Church, the whole people of God, called and committed to his service. He equips them with particular gifts and calls some to the ministry of the Word and Sacraments and some to be elders. Elders share with the minister in the pastoral oversight and leadership of the local church.

Today we are to

ordain to the eldership of the United Reformed Church ABC *and to induct* him/her/them *(together with* OPQ) *to serve in this congregation.*

induct OPQ *to the eldership in this congregation.*

First, let us be reminded of the Nature, Faith, and Order of our church.

The Statement concerning the Nature, Faith, and Order of the United Reformed Church is read in one of the approved forms.

2. Affirmations by those to be Ordained

The minister invites the whole congregation to stand and then addresses those to be ordained.

In the light of this statement, do you confess again your faith in one God, Father, Son, and Holy Spirit?

I do.

In dependence on God's grace do you reaffirm your trust in Jesus Christ as Saviour and Lord, and your promise to follow him and to seek to do and to bear his will all the days of your life?

I do.

Do you believe that the Word of God in the Old and New Testaments, discerned under the guidance of the Holy Spirit, is the supreme authority for the faith and conduct of all God's people?

I do.

3. The Ordination

The minister and those elders appointed to lay hands on those to be ordained do so, ordaining them one at a time. Those to be ordained kneel for the ordination.

Almighty God our Father, we thank you for giving us women and men of faith and integrity and calling them to your service. In your name and in obedience to your will, we now ordain *AB* to be an elder in your Church. Enrich *him/her* with the Holy Spirit: give *him/her* grace to be faithful in *his/her* work, for Jesus Christ's sake.

Amen.

The newly ordained elders stand

In the name of the Lord Jesus Christ, the only head of the Church, and in accordance with the decisions of this church, I declare *ABC* to be ordained elder(s) in the United Reformed Church.

The newly ordained elders do not respond to the next two questions.

4. The Induction

I now call upon you, elders and members of this congregation, to dedicate yourselves anew to Christ and to the task of ministry which he lays upon us all, responding with the words: 'We do.'

Do you confess again your faith in Jesus Christ as Saviour and Lord?
We do.

Do you seek to fulfil together your common calling to the glory of the one God, Father, Son, and Holy Spirit?
We do.

The minister addresses all the elders who are to be inducted:

ABC, OPQ do you accept the office of elder in this congregation and promise to perform its duties faithfully, God being your helper?
I do.

And do you, members of this congregation, promise to support and encourage those you have elected and support them in your prayers?
We do.

A prayer such as the following is offered for the new elders by the minister. The elders being inducted remain standing; the congregation may sit.

Almighty God our Father, we seek your blessing on these your servants. Grant them vision and courage in leading this church in its witness in the world. Give them the mind of Christ to seek peace and unity, and the heart of Christ to rejoice with those that rejoice and weep with those that weep. Deepen their knowledge of yourself and may they reflect your love; through Jesus Christ our Lord.
Amen.

In the name of the Lord Jesus Christ, the only head of the Church, and in accordance with the decision of this church, I declare that you are inducted to the office of elder in this church, in token of which we give you the right hand of fellowship.

The minister and others give the right hand of fellowship.

The almighty God and Father grant you his grace that in this your charge you may be found faithful.

Scripture Readings

OLD TESTAMENT

Exod. 18: 13–27; Num. 11: 16–17, 24–30; Isa. 42: 1–9, Ezek. 34: 11–16.

NEW TESTAMENT

Matt. 25: 14–28; Mark 10: 35–45; Luke 12: 35–40; John 4: 31–8; 10: 1–6, 10b–18; 21: 15–17; Acts 20: 28–35; Rom. 12: 1–18; 1 Corinthians 3: 5–11; 12: 4–13; Eph. 4: 1–16; Phil. 2: 1–3; 1 Peter 4: 7–11; 5: 1–4.

COMMISSIONING OF ACCREDITED LAY PREACHERS

1. Introduction
2. Statement
3. The Affirmations
4. The Commissioning
5. Declaration
6. Presentation

The commissioning is conducted by the District Council (after accreditation by the Council) either at an ordinary meeting of the Council or at a special service, perhaps at the lay preacher's own church. In the latter case representatives of the District Council will be present and participating; in the former case representatives of the local church or churches will be present and participating, and family and friends are invited.

The service may begin with the Call to Worship. Prayer(s), Scripture Reading(s), Sermon or Charge, and a Hymn or Hymns. Appropriate readings are appended to this order.

1. Introduction

In the name of the Lord Jesus Christ, the head of the Church, we meet to commission as a *lay preacher/lay preachers*: *AB, CD* . . . who *has/have* been accredited by the *XY* District Council.

2. Statement

An opportunity may be made for the lay preacher(s) to make a statement concerning their faith and sense of calling.

3. The Affirmations

The congregation is invited to stand.

Let us hear *AB, CD* . . . reaffirm *his/her/their* faith and express the intention to exercise this ministry.

Do you confess again your faith in one God, Father, Son, and Holy Spirit?
I do.

In dependence on God's grace, do you reaffirm your trust in Jesus Christ as Saviour and Lord, and your promise to follow him and to seek to do and to bear his will all the days of your life?
I do.

Do you believe that the Word of God in the Old and New Testaments, discerned under the guidance of the Holy Spirit, is the supreme authority for the faith and conduct of all God's people?
I do.

Do you believe that you are called to preach the gospel of God's love and mercy revealed in Jesus Christ?
I do.

Do you undertake to exercise your ministry in accordance with the Nature, Faith, and Order of the United Reformed Church?
I do.

Do you, members of *LM* church and *XY* District Council, accept *AB*, *CD* . . . as (an) accredited lay preacher(s) and promise *him/her/them* your prayerful support and encouragement in this ministry?
We do.

4. The Commissioning

The lay preacher(s) may kneel and appropriate persons may lay hands on each one

A prayer such as the following may be used

Most merciful God and Father,
you have set your Church in the world,
to bear witness to the gospel,
and you equip it with the gifts it needs.
We thank you that once again,
you have given us living proof of the way you call
disciples into new realms of service.

In your name we commission *AB*, *CD* . . . to the office of lay
   preacher in your Church,
praying that you will enrich your servant(s) with the Holy Spirit.
Give *him/her/them* grace to be faithful in the work.
Lead *him/her/them* ever deeper into understanding of the gospel,
   and sustain *his/her/their* sense of calling to proclaim it.
Through this ministry may men and women be reconciled to
   yourself and grow up in Christ.
In his name we pray.
   Amen.

Those kneeling stand up

5. Declaration

In the Name of the Lord Jesus Christ, the only head of the Church, and in accordance with the decision of the District Council, I declare you to be commissioned to the office of lay preacher in the United Reformed Church.
I therefore give you the right hand of fellowship.

6. Presentation

The certificate and also a Bible or other suitable gift may be presented to each lay preacher

The service may conclude with Holy Communion

Scripture Readings

OLD TESTAMENT

Num. 11: 16–17, 24–30; Isa. 52: 7–12; Jer. 23: 16–22; Ezek. 3: 16–21

NEW TESTAMENT

Matt. 9: 33–10: 15; 28: 16–20; Luke 10: 1–20; John 15: 1–17; Acts 11: 19–26; Rom. 1: 8–17; 10: 5–17; 2 Cor. 5: 11–6: 2

SERVICE FOR HEALING

1. Welcome
2. Scripture Sentences
3. Prayer of Approach
4. Prayer of Confession
5. Scripture Reading(s)
6. Sermon
7. Offertory
8. Prayers of Thanksgiving and Intercession
9. The Laying on of Hands
10. Final Prayer
11. Dismissal and Blessing

Introductory Notes

The use of a Service for Healing provides a valuable means of expressing the Church's concern for a salvation which relates to the whole person, body, mind, and spirit, and to the community.

Services for healing will vary in content and order according to local circumstances. Services in a home will probably not take exactly the same form as those conducted in the formal setting of a church building. Wherever the service is held, adequate time for quiet meditation should be provided, so that it is clear that an important aspect of worship is quiet waiting upon God.

Where the laying on of hands is included, it is recommended that it should be carefully introduced to avoid misunderstanding. It is also advisable that it should be given not only by the minister(s) but also by others. It then becomes clear that the healing ministry is not the prerogative of any one person but the responsibility and privilege of the whole church.

Some Practical Suggestions

*a) **Welcome***

The leader should explain that the service is one of praise and openness to God and that healing will be part of this. As worshippers make their requests known to God, so he will make known his will to them in his own way and in his own time.

HEALING SERVICE

b) **Prayers**
   i) *Responsive prayers are a valuable means of involving the whole congregation.*
   ii) *The names of those who have asked for prayer may be mentioned during the intercessions.*
   iii) *Brief prayers or biblical texts might be made available for members of the congregation to use whilst the laying on of hands is taking place.*

c) **The laying on of hands**
   People wishing to receive the laying on of hands should be invited to come and sit or kneel at the front of the church.

   The invitation is probably best offered in the broadest terms to indicate that what we are concerned about is wholeness in its fullest sense of being completely reconciled to God.

   After the invitation to come forward is given, a hymn may be sung or an organ voluntary played whilst those wishing for this ministry move forward. People may be invited to articulate briefly their own need and also their concern for others. Prayer will then be offered with the laying on of hands.

d) **The Communion Service**
   The service for healing may appropriately take place within the context of Holy Communion.

e) **Anointing**
   There has been a re-discovery of the ancient practice of anointing with oil those who are sick. It should be made plain that this can be made available, though it should perhaps be used more selectively and privately than the laying on of hands. It can quite naturally take place alongside the laying on of hands for those who specially request it. It is helpful if prior notice is given when this is required.

   Anointing is usually with olive oil carried in a suitable container. The thumb of the right hand is dipped into the oil and then placed on the forehead with prayer, making the sign of the cross. Some choose also to have the palms of the hands anointed in the same way.

HEALING SERVICE

1. Welcome

2. Scripture Sentences

The Lord is at hand. Have no anxiety about anything but in everything by prayer and supplication with thanksgiving let your requests be made known to God. And the peace of God, which passes all understanding, will keep your hearts and your minds in Christ Jesus. *Phil. 4: 5–7*

3. Prayer of Approach

Almighty God, you called your Church to witness that in Christ all things are reconciled to yourself; help us so to proclaim the good news of your love, that all who hear it may be reconciled to you; through him who died for us and rose again and reigns with you and the Holy Spirit, one God, now and for ever.
 Amen.

or (2)

Almighty God,
to whom all hearts are open,
all desires known,
and from whom no secrets are hidden:
cleanse the thoughts of our hearts
by the inspiration of your Holy Spirit,
that we may perfectly love you,
and worthily magnify your holy name;
through Christ our Lord.
 Amen.

4. Prayer of Confession

Almighty God, we confess that, like sheep, we have gone astray; we are tired of missing your way and stumbling along paths of our own choosing. We come back to you like sheep to the fold. We confess that we are not proud of the mistakes we have made or of the failures that hang over us like a cloud.

We seek now your forgiveness for our blindness and our folly, for what we have done and for what we have failed to do. Forgive our lack of faith, our laziness in prayer, our unreadiness to have our lives disturbed or our self-indulgence challenged by the gospel.

For the sake of your son, Jesus Christ, forgive us all that is past, confirm and strengthen us in faith and hope and bring us to refreshment and renewal in him.
Amen.

or

Father eternal, giver of light and grace, we have sinned against you and against each other, in what we have thought, in what we have said and done, through ignorance, through weakness, through our own deliberate fault. We have wounded your love and marred your image in us.

We are sorry and ashamed. We repent of all our sins. For the sake of your Son, Jesus Christ, who died for us, forgive us all that is past; and lead us out from darkness to walk as children of light.
Amen.

or (3a)

**Lord God most merciful,
we confess that we have sinned,
through our own fault,
and in common with others,
in thought, word, and deed,
and through what we have left undone.**

**We ask to be forgiven.
By the power of your Spirit
turn us from evil to good,
help us to forgive others,
and keep us in your ways
of righteousness and love;
through Jesus Christ our Lord. Amen.**

To all who confess their sins and resolve to lead a new life, Jesus says: 'Your sins are forgiven.' He also says: 'Follow me.' Now to the King of all worlds, immortal, invisible, the only wise God, be honour and glory for ever and ever.
Amen.

5. Scripture Reading(s)

6. Sermon

followed by silent meditation

7. Offertory

8. Prayers of Thanksgiving and Intercession

Lord God, our Father, accept our thanks for everything that speaks to us of your love, enriches our lives, and gives purpose to our days. We give thanks for the world of nature, providing so much for our bodily needs; for home, for family and friends; for tasks to do and the satisfaction that comes from those well done.

We give thanks for the coming of your Son to live our life and to grant us victory over sin and death; for his teaching, preaching, and healing whereby he declared your loving care and revealed your power to heal and save.

We rejoice in the gift of your Spirit who gives life to the world, guides us in our perplexities, comforts us in our sorrows, and quickens us to respond to your Word. We give thanks for the Church in every age, remembering those who have handed down to us such a rich heritage of witness and service.

Help us in our day to continue steadfast, courageous and true to you, our ever-living Lord, that everyone may rejoice to see your power at work in us; through Jesus Christ our Lord.
Amen.

Intercessions and The Lord's Prayer

9. The Laying on of Hands

An invitation may be given to those wishing for the laying on of hands to come forward: for assurance of forgiveness; commitment to Christ; healing of the body, mind and spirit; help for themselves or for others in facing personal problems. The congregation may be encouraged to sit quietly in prayer and to meditate upon a verse of scripture, e.g.:

'I am the Lord, the one who heals you.'
Jesus said: 'It is my own peace that I give you.'

or upon a prayer:

Lord Jesus, the same yesterday, today and for ever, let your healing power be upon those who seek your help at this time. Grant them new life and strength.

Opportunity may now be given to those coming forward to speak of their need. An extempore prayer may be offered, or one of the following:

A . . ., in the name of God the Father, may new life quicken you in body, mind, and spirit. In the name of Jesus Christ, may you be made whole in him. In the name of the Holy Spirit, may you be given that peace which passes understanding.

or

A . . ., may the Lord Christ grant you healing and renewal, according to his will. Go in peace.

10. Final Prayer

We praise and thank you, our God, that in Jesus Christ you have given us life and brought forgiveness and healing to us. Continue, we pray, your healing work among us and keep us ever mindful of your love and mercy, that we may be faithful throughout all our days, to the honour and glory of Jesus Christ, our Lord.
Amen.

11. Dismissal and Blessing

Scripture Readings

OLD TESTAMENT

Pss. 23; 27; 30; 43; 46; 51; 86; 91; 103; 116; 121; 139; 143 (omit v. 12).
Isa. 40: 1–11; 53: 4–12; 54: 7–10; 58: 1, 6, 9.

NEW TESTAMENT

Matt. 5: 1–12; 6: 25–34. Mark 1: 21–34; 2: 1–12; 9: 14–29. Luke 7: 18–23; 9: 1–6; 10: 1–9, 38–42; 11: 5–13. John 9; 14: 12–17. Acts 3: 1–16; 28: 7–10. 2 Cor. 12: 7–10. Jas. 5: 13–16.

THE LORD'S PRAYER

Modern Form

Our Father in heaven,
hallowed be your name,
your kingdom come,
your will be done,
on earth as in heaven.
Give us today our daily bread.
Forgive us our sins
as we forgive those who sin against us.
Save us from the time of trial
and deliver us from evil.

For the kingdom, the power, and the glory are yours,
now and for ever.
Amen.

Traditional Form

Our Father, who art in heaven,
hallowed be thy name;
thy kingdom come;
thy will be done;
on earth as it is in heaven.
Give us this day our daily bread.
And forgive us our trespasses,
as we forgive those who trespass against us.
And lead us not into temptation,
but deliver us from evil.

For thine is the kingdom,
the power, and the glory,
for ever and ever.
Amen.

CREEDS

The Apostles' Creed

I believe in God, the Father almighty,
 creator of heaven and earth.

I believe in Jesus Christ, God's only Son, our Lord,
 who was conceived by the Holy Spirit,
 born of the Virgin Mary,
 suffered under Pontius Pilate,
 was crucified, died, and was buried;
 he descended to the dead.
 On the third day he rose again;
 he ascended into heaven.
 He is seated at the right hand of the Father,
 and he will come again to judge the living and the dead.

I believe in the Holy Spirit,
 the holy catholic Church,
 the communion of saints,
 the forgiveness of sins,
 the resurrection of the body,
 and the life everlasting. **Amen.**

The Nicene Creed

We believe in one God,
 the Father, the Almighty,
 maker of heaven and earth,
 of all that is, seen and unseen.
We believe in one Lord, Jesus Christ,
 the only son of God,
 eternally begotten of the Father,
 God from God, Light from Light,
 true God from true God,
 begotten, not made,
 of one Being with the Father;
 through him all things were made.

For us and for our salvation
> he came down from heaven,
> was incarnate of the Holy Spirit and the Virgin Mary
> and became truly human.
> For our sake he was crucified under Pontius Pilate;
> he suffered death and was buried.
> On the third day he rose again
> in accordance with the Scriptures;
> he ascended into heaven
> and is seated at the right hand of the Father.
> He will come again in glory to judge the living and the dead,
> and his kingdom will have no end.

We believe in the Holy Spirit, the Lord, the giver of life,
> who proceeds from the Father (and the Son),
> who with the Father and the Son is worshipped and glorified,
> who has spoken through the Prophets.
> We believe in one, holy, catholic, and apostolic Church.
> We acknowledge one baptism for the forgiveness of sins.
> We look for the resurrection of the dead,
> and the life of the world to come. **Amen.**

CONFESSION OF FAITH

We believe in one living and true God,
creator, preserver and ruler of all things in heaven and earth,
 Father, Son and Holy Spirit:
 Him alone we worship, and in him we put our trust.

We believe that God, in his infinite love for all,
gave his eternal Son, Jesus Christ our Lord,
who became man,
lived on earth in perfect love and obedience,
died upon the cross for our sins,
rose again from the dead:
 And lives for evermore, saviour, judge, and king.

We believe that, by the Holy Spirit,
this glorious gospel is made effective
so that through faith we receive the forgiveness of sins,
newness of life as children of God
and strength in this present world to do his will.
We believe in one, holy, catholic, apostolic Church,
in heaven and on earth,
wherein by the same Spirit,
the whole company of believers is made one Body of Christ:
 To worship God and serve him and all in his kingdom of righteousness and love.
 We rejoice in the gift of eternal life, and believe that, in the fullness of time,
 God will renew and gather in one all things in Christ,
 to whom with the Father and the Holy Spirit,
 be glory and majesty, dominion and power,
 both now and ever. **Amen.**

A variation on the *Confession of Faith of the United Reformed Church* as printed in *THE MANUAL*.

STATEMENT CONCERNING THE NATURE, FAITH, AND ORDER OF THE UNITED REFORMED CHURCH

With the whole Christian Church
the United Reformed Church believes in one God,
Father, Son, and Holy Spirit.

> **The living God, the only God,
> ever to be praised.**

The life of faith to which we are called
is the Spirit's gift
continually received
through the Word, the Sacraments,
and our Christian life together.

> **We acknowledge the gift
> and answer the call,
> giving thanks for the means of grace**

The highest authority
for what we believe and do
is God's Word in the Bible
alive for his people today
through the help of the Spirit.

> **We respond to this Word,
> whose servants we are
> with all God's people
> through the years.**

We accept with thanksgiving to God
the witness to the catholic faith
in the Apostles' and Nicene creeds.
We acknowledge the declarations
made in our own tradition

by Congregationalists, Presbyterians,
and Churches of Christ
in which they stated the faith
and sought to make its implications clear.

> **Faith alive and active:**
> **gift of an eternal source,**
> **renewed for every generation.**

We conduct our life together
according to the Basis of Union
in which we give expression to our faith
in forms which we believe contain
the essential elements of the Church's life,
both catholic and reformed;
but we affirm our right and readiness,
if the need arises,
to change the Basis of Union
and to make new statements of faith
in ever new obedience to the Living Christ.

> **Our crucified and risen Lord,**
> **who leads us in our faith**
> **and brings it to perfection.**

Held together in the Body of Christ
through the freedom of the Spirit,
we rejoice in the diversity of the Spirit's gifts
and uphold the rights of personal conviction.
For the sake of faith and fellowship
it shall be for the Church to decide
when differences of conviction
hurt our unity and peace.

> **We commit ourselves**
> **to speak the truth in love**
> **and grow together**
> **in the peace of Christ.**

We believe that
Christ gives his Church a government
distinct from the government of the state.

STATEMENT OF UNITED REFORMED CHURCH

In things that affect obedience to God
the Church is not subordinate to the state,
but must serve the Lord Jesus Christ,
its only King and Head.
Civil authorities are called
to serve God's will of justice and peace for
all humanity,
and to respect the rights of conscience and belief.

> **While we ourselves
> are servants in the world,
> as citizens of God's eternal kingdom**

We affirm our intention
to go on praying and working,
with all our fellow Christians
for the visible unity of the Church
in the way Christ chooses,
so that people and nations
may be led to love and serve God
and praise him more and more for ever.

> **Source, Guide, and Goal
> of all that is:
> to him be eternal glory.**

Amen.

CALENDAR AND LECTIONARY

The scripture readings are based on the work of the Joint Liturgical Group.

In the left-hand column are those for the first year cycle and in the centre those for the second year. The psalms in the third column apply to either year.

The first cycle begins when the ninth Sunday before Christmas falls in a year with an even number (e.g. 1990) whilst the second cycle begins in the years with odd numbers.

* indicates the main or controlling reading for the day.

† indicates psalm, metrical psalm, metrical psalm/hymn or canticle, will be found in the companion hymn book.

YEAR 1   **YEAR 2**

9 Christmas

*Gen. 1: 1–3, 24–31a   *Gen. 2: 4b–9, 15–25   Pss. †8;
Col. 1: 15–20   Rev: 4   104: 1–10
John 1: 1–14   John 3: 1–8

8 Christmas

*Gen. 4: 1–10   *Gen. 3: 1–15   Pss. 86;
1 John 3: 9–18   Rom. 7: 7–13   †130
Mark 7: 14–23   John 3: 13–21

7 Christmas

*Gen. 12: 1–9   *Gen. 22: 1–18   Pss. †1;
Rom. 4: 13–25   Jas. 2: 14–24   105: 1–11
John 8: 51–8   Luke 20: 9–17

6 Christmas

*Exod. 3: 7–15   *Exod. 6: 2–8   Pss. 77: 11– end;
Heb. 3: 1–6   Heb. 11: 17–31   106: 1–14, 39–48;
John 6: 25–35   Mark 13: 5–13   †111

5 Christmas

*1 Kings 19: 9–18   *Isa. 10: 20–3   Pss. †80: 1–7
Rom. 11: 13–24   Rom. 9: 19–28   †130
Matt. 24: 37–44   Mark 13: 14–23   †Salvator Mundi

4 Christmas (Advent 1)

*Isa. 52: 7–10	*Isa. 51: 4–11	Pss. †96;
1 Thess. 5: 1–11	Rom. 13: 8–14	†98
Luke 21: 25–33	Matt. 25: 31–46	

3 Christmas (Advent 2)
Bible Sunday

*Isa. 55: 1–11	*Isa. 64: 1–7	Pss. †19;
2 Tim. 3: 14–4:5	Rom. 15: 4–13	119: 33–40; 119:
John 5: 36b–47	Luke 4: 14–21	129–136

2 Christmas (Advent 3)

*Isa. 40: 1–11	*Mal. 3: 1–5	Ps. 126;
1 Cor. 4: 1–5	Phil. 4: 4–9	†Benedictus
John 1: 19–28	Matt. 11: 2–15	

1 Christmas (Advent 4)

*Isa. 11: 1–9	*Zech. 2: 10– end	†Magnificat
1 Cor. 1: 26– end	Rev. 21: 1–7	Ps. †131
Luke 1: 26–38a	Matt. 1: 18–23	

Christmas Eve and Christmas Day

*Isa. 9: 2,6–7/Isa. 62: 10–12/Mic. 5: 2–4   Pss. †85;
Titus 2: 11–14; 3: 3–7/1 John 4: 7–14/Heb. 1:   †98
1–15
*Luke 2: 1–14 (15–20)/Luke 2: 8–20/John 1:1–14

Christmas 1

Isa. 7: 10–14	1 Sam. 1: 20–8	Pss. †8; †116: 13,
Gal. 4: 1–7	Rom. 12: 1–8	14: 17–19; 122
*John 1: 14–18	*Luke 2: 21–40	

Christmas 2

Ecclus. 3: 2–7/ Exod.	Isa. 60: 1–6	†Nunc Dimittis
12: 21–7	Rev. 21: 22–22.5	Ps. †72: 1–19
Rom. 8: 11–17	*Matt. 2: 1–12, 19–23	
*Luke 2: 41– end		

Some years this has to be omitted

Epiphany (6 January)

Isa. 49: 1–6   Ps. †72; 1–19

CALENDAR AND LECTIONARY

Eph. 3: 1–12
*Matt. 2: 1–12

Christmas 3/1 Epiphany 1

1 Sam. 16: 1–13a	Isa. 42: 1–7	Pss. †36: 5–10;
Acts 10: 34–8a	Eph. 2: 1–10	89: 19–30
*Matt. 3: 13– end	*John 1: 29–34	

Christmas 4/Epiphany 2

Jer. 1: 4–10	1 Sam. 3: 1–10	Pss. †145; †67;
Acts 26: 1, 9–20	Gal. 1: 11– end	†100
*Mark 1: 14–20	*John 1: 35– end	

Christmas 5/Epiphany 3

Exod. 33: 12– end	Deut. 8: 1–6	Pss. †46; †107:
1 John 1: 1–7	Phil. 4: 10–20	1–32;
*John 2: 1–11	*John 6: 1–14	119: 1–16

Christmas 6/Epiphany 4

1 Kings 8: 22–30	Jer. 7: 1–11	Pss. †84; †34
1 Cor. 3: 10–17	Heb. 12: 18– end	
*John 2: 13–22	*John 4: 19–26	

Christmas 7/Epiphany 5

Prov. 2: 1–9/	2 Sam. 12: 1–10, 13	Pss. †100; †36:
Ecclus. 42: 15– end		5–10; 49: 1–12;
1 Cor. 3: 18– end	Rom. 1: 18–25	†116: 1–9; 138
*Matt. 12: 38–42	*Matt. 13: 24–30	

Christmas 8/Epiphany 6

Years 1 and 2	Isa. 1: 10–17	Pss. †25: 1–10; †43:
	Acts 16: 11–15	3–5;
	*Mark 2: 23–3: 6	

9 Easter

Isa. 30: 18–21	Prov. 3: 1–8	Ps. †103
1 Cor. 4: 8–13	1 Cor. 2: 1–10	†The Beatitudes
*Matt. 5: 1–12	*Luke 8: 4–15	

8 Easter

Zeph. 3: 14– end	2 Kings 5: 1–14	Pss. †131; †46
Jas. 5: 13–16a	2 Cor. 12: 1–10	
*Mark 2: 1–12	*Mark 7: 24– end	

7 Easter

Hosea 14: 1–7	Num. 15: 32–6	Pss. †139
Philemon: 1–16	Col. 1: 18–23	32; 66
*Mark 2: 13–17	*John 8: 2–11	

Ash Wednesday

Isa. 58: 1–8/Joel 2: 12–17/Amos 5: 6–16
1 Cor. 9: 24– end/Jas. 4: 1–10
*Matt. 6: 16–21/Luke 18: 9–14

Pss. †51: 1–17; †130

6 Easter/Lent 1

Gen. 2: 7–9; 3: 1–7	Gen. 4: 1–10	Pss. †51: 1–17;
Heb. 2: 14– end	Heb. 4: 12– end	†91: 1–16
*Matt. 4: 1–11	*Luke 4: 1–13	

5 Easter/Lent 2

Gen. 6: 11– end	Gen. 7: 17– end	Pss. †18: 1–6;
1John 4: 1–6	1 John 3: 1–10	16–19; 119: 33–40
*Luke 19: 41– end	*Matt. 12: 22–32	

4 Easter/Lent 3

Gen. 22: 1–13	Gen. 12: 1–9	Pss. †42; 115: 1–10;
Col. 1: 24– end	1 Pet. 2: 19–25	55
*Luke 9: 18–27	*Matt. 16: 13– end	

3 Easter/Lent 4

Exod. 34: 29– end	Exod. 3: 1–6	Pss. †84; †36: 5–10
2 Cor. 3: 4– end	2 Pet. 1: 16–19	
*Luke 9: 28–36	*Matt. 17: 1–13	

2 Easter/Lent 5

Exod. 6: 2–13	Jer. 31: 31–4	Pss. †22: 1–21; 143:
Col. 2: 8–15	Heb. 9: 11–14	1–11
*John 12: 20–32	*Mark 10: 32–45	

CALENDAR AND LECTIONARY

1 Easter/Palm Sunday

Isa. 50: 4–9a	Zech. 9: 9–12	Pss. †24; †22: 1–21
Phil. 2: 5–11	*or* 1 Cor. 1: 18–25	
*Mark 14: 32–15: 4	*Matt. 21: 1–13	

Maundy Thursday

Exod. 12: 1–14	Jer. 31: 31–4	Pss. †116; 26: 6–8
1 Cor. 11: 23–32	1 Cor. 10: 16–17	
*John 13: 1–17	*Mark 14: 12–26	

Good Friday

Isa. 52: 13–53; end
Heb. 10: 11–25/Heb. 4: 14–5: 9
*John 18: 1–19: 37/John 19: 1–37

Pss. †22: 1–21; 40; †40: 1–4; 69: 17–23

Easter Day

Gen. 1: 1–15, 26–8, 31/Exod. 4: 27–5: 1/Exod. 14: 21–31/Isa. 12/Isa. 43: 16–21
Rom. 6: 3–11/1 Cor. 15: 12–20/Col. 3: 1–11/ Rev. 1: 10–18
*Matt. 28: 1–10/*John 20: 1–10 (*or* 18)/ *Mark 16: 1–8

Ps. †118: 14–29
†Te Deum

Easter 1

Exod. 15: 1–11	Exod. 16: 2–15	Pss. †145: 1–21
1 Pet. 1: 3–9	1 Cor. 15: 53– end	hymn versions: †150
*John 20: 19–29	*John 6: 32–40	

Easter 2

Isa. 25: 6–9	Ezek. 34: 7–16	Pss. 11; †23
Rev. 16: 6–9	1 Pet. 5: 1–11	
*Luke 24: 13–35	*Jonn 10: 7–16	

Easter 3

Isa. 61: 1–7	1 Kings 17: 17– end	Pss. †27; 16
1 Cor. 15: 1–11	Col. 3: 1–11	
*John 21: 1–14	*John 11: 17–27	

Easter 4

Isa. 62: 1–5	Prov. 4: 10–19	Pss. †98; 37: 23–32
Rev. 3: 14– end	2 Cor. 4: 13–5: 5	
*John 21: 15–22	*John 14: 1–11	

Easter 5

Hosea 6: 1–6	Deut. 34	Pss. †65; 124
1 Cor. 15: 21–8	Rom. 8: 28– end	
*John 16: 25– end	*John 16: 12–24	

Ascension Day

Dan. 7: 9–14
Acts 1: 1–11
*Matt. 28: 16– end

Pss. †8; †24; 68

Easter 6

Dan. 7: 9–14	2 Kings 2: 1–14	Pss. †47; †24
Eph. 1: 15– end	Eph. 4: 1–13	
*Luke 24: 45– end	*Luke 24: 45– end	

Pentecost

Gen. 11: 1–9/Exod. 19: 16–25
*Acts 2: 1–11 (*or* 21)
John 14: 15–26/John 20: 19–23

Pss. †122; †104; †98
†122

Pentecost 1/Trinity

Isa. 6: 1–8	Deut. 6: 4–9	Ps. 97
*Eph. 1: 3–14	*Acts 2: 22–4	†Trisagion
John 14: 8–17	(*or* 31) 32–6	
	Matt. 11: 25–30	

Pentecost 2

Exod. 19: 1–6	2 Sam. 7: 4–16	†Venite
*1 Pet. 2: 1–10	*Acts 2: 37– end	Pss. 133; 135: 1–6
John 15: 1–5	Luke 14: 15–24	

Pentecost 3

Deut. 6: 17– end	Deut. 8: 11– end	Pss. †84; 78; 102
*Rom. 6: 3–11	*Acts 4: 8–12	
John 15: 5–11	Luke 8: 41– end	

CALENDAR AND LECTIONARY

Pentecost 4

Deut. 7: 6–11	Isa. 63: 7–14	Pss. †63; 147
*Gal. 3: 23–4: 7	*Acts 8: 26–38	
John 15: 12–17	Luke 15: 1–10	

Pentecost 5

Exod. 20: 1–17	Ruth 1: 8–17, 22	Pss. †100; †96
*Eph. 5: 1–10	*Acts 11: 4–18	
Matt. 19: 16–26	Luke 10: 1–12	

Pentecost 6

Exod. 24: 3–11	Micah 6: 1–8	Pss. †121; 112
*Col. 3: 12–17	*Eph. 4: 17–32	
Luke 15: 11– end	Mark 10: 46– end	

Pentecost 7

Hosea 11: 1–9	Deut. 10: 12–11.1	Pss. †62; 99
*1 Cor. 12: 27–13: end	*Rom. 8: 1–11	
Matt. 18: 21–35	Mark 12: 28–34	

Pentecost 8

Ezek. 36: 24–8	Ezek. 37: 1–14	Pss. †25: 1–10; †148
*Gal. 5: 16–25	*1 Cor. 12: 4–13	
John 15: 16– end	Luke 6: 27–38	

Pentecost 9

Josh. 1: 1–9	1 Sam. 17: 37–50	Pss. †18: 1–6;
*Eph. 6: 10–20	*2 Cor. 6: 3–10	16–19; 9
John 17: 11b–19	Mark 9: 14–29	

Pentecost 10

Job 42: 1–6	1 Sam. 24: 9–17	Pss. †19; 4
*Phil. 2: 1–11	(*or* 1–17)	
John 13: 1–15	*Gal. 6: 1–10	
	Luke 7: 36– end	

Pentecost 11

Isa. 42: 1–7	1 Chron. 29: 1–9	Pss. †145; 31: 1–6
*2 Cor. 4: 1–10	*Phil. 1: 1–11	
John 13: 31–5	Matt. 20: 1–16	

Pentecost 12

Isa. 49: 1–6	Micah 4: 1–5	Pss. †98; †150
*2 Cor. 5: 14–6: 2	*Acts 17: 22– end	
John 17: 20– end	Matt. 5: 13–16	

Pentecost 13

Isa. 50: 4–9a	Jer. 20: 7–11a	Pss. †43; 31: 3–5
*Acts 7: 54–8.1	*Acts 20: 17–35	
John 16: 1–11	Matt. 10: 16–22	

Pentecost 14

Prov. 31: 10– end	Gen. 45: 1–15	Pss. †103;
*Eph. 5: 25–6: 4	*Eph. 3: 14– end	127; 128
Mark 10: 2–16	Luke 11: 1–13	

Pentecost 15

Isa. 45: 1–7	1 Kings 3: 4–15	Pss. †20; 50;
*Rom. 13: 1–7	*1 Tim. 2: 1–7	†80: 1–7
Matt. 22: 15–22	Matt. 14: 1–12	

Pentecost 16

Lev. 19: 9–18	Deut. 15: 7–11	Pss. †34: 1–18;
*Rom. 12: 9– end	*1 John 4: 15– end	†107: 1–9
Luke 10: 25–37	Luke 16: 19– end	

Pentecost 17

Jer. 7: 1–11	Jer. 32: 6–15	Pss. †27; 57; 92
*Jas. 1: 16– end	*Gal. 2: 15–3:9	
Luke 17: 11–19	Luke 7: 1–10	

Pentecost 18

Deut. 26: 1–11	Neh. 6: 1–16/	Pss. †145: 8–21;
	Ecclus. 38: 24– end	†90
*2 Cor. 8: 1–9	*1 Pet. 4: 7–11	
Matt. 5: 17–26	Matt. 25: 14–30	

Pentecost 19

Gen. 28: 10– end	Dan. 6: 10–23	Pss. †139: 1–24;
*Heb. 11: 1–2, 8–16	*Rom. 5: 1–11	†103
Matt. 6: 24– end	Luke 19: 1–10	

CALENDAR AND LECTIONARY

Pentecost 20

Dan. 3: 13–26	Gen. 32: 22–30	Pss. †121; 39
*Rom. 8: 18–25	*1 Cor. 9: 19– end	
Luke 9: 51– end	Matt. 7: 13–27	

Pentecost 21

Hab. 2: 1–4	Ezek. 12: 21– end	Pss. 71: 1–8;
*Acts 26: 1–8	*1 Pet. 1: 12–31	61
Luke 18: 1–8	John 11: 17–27	†Te Deum

Pentecost 22

(*Years 1 and 2*) Deut. 11: 18–28   Pss. †1; †42
*1 John 2: 22– end
Luke 16: 1–9

Last Sunday after Pentecost

Jer. 29: 1, 4–14	Isa. 33: 17–22	Pss. †146; 15
*Phil. 3: 7– end	*Rev. 7: 2–4, 9–17	
John 17: 1–10	Matt. 25: 1–13	

Remembrance (Peace) Sunday

Isa. 52: 7–12/Micah 4: 3–5/2 Sam. 23: 13–17   Pss. †46; †72: 1–19
Rev. 22: 1–5/1 Tim. 2: 1–5/Rom. 8: 31–5, 37–9
John 15: 9–17/Matt. 5: 43– end/Matt. 5: 1–12

Church Unity

Jer. 33: 6–9a/Deut. 6: 4–9/Isa. 11: 1–9   Pss. †122; 133
Eph. 4: 1–6 or 16/Eph. 2: 11–22/1 Cor. 3: 1–11   †Te Deum
John 17: 11b–23/John 17: 20–6/John 15: 1–11

World Mission

Isa. 42: 1–9/Isa. 49: 1–6/Isa. 52: 7–10   Pss. †67; †117
Rom. 1: 8–17/Acts 16: 1–10/Rom. 10: 5–17
John 3: 1–16/Matt. 28: 16–20/Luke 10: 1–9

All Saints

Jer. 31: 31–4/Isa. 66: 20–3   Pss. †145; 15
Heb. 11: 32–12: 2 (18–24)/Rev. 7: 2–4, 9–12
Matt. 5: 1–11 (12)/Luke 6: 20–3

Church Anniversary

2 Chron. 7: 11–16/1 Kings 8: 22–30/   Pss. †84; 134
Gen. 28: 10–22
Heb. 10: 19–25/1 Pet. 2: 1–5/Rev. 21: 9–14, 22–7
John 10: 22–9/Matt. 21: 12–16/Matt. 12: 1–21

Civic and Social Responsibility

Deut. 5: 1–21/Amos 5: 21–4/Isa. 58: 1–8   Pss. †72: 5–19; †146
Phil. 2: 1–11/Acts 5: 1–11/Rom. 14: 1–9   Mark 10: 42–5
                                                                       Matt 25: 31- end
                                                                       Matt 5: 43– end

Harvest

Gen. 8: 15–22/Deut. 8: 1–10/Deut. 26: 1–11   Pss. †65; †24;
Rev. 14: 14–18/Acts 14: 13–17/1 Tim. 6: 6–10   †145: 1–21
Mark 4: 1–9/Luke 12: 16–31/Matt: 13.24–33

New Year

Josh. 1: 6–9   Pss. †91: 1–16; †103
Phil. 3: 9–17
Matt. 6: 19–34

ACKNOWLEDGEMENTS

AN ORDER OF WORSHIP

The English translation of 'Gloria in Excelsis', originally prepared by the International Consultation on English texts and revised in 1987 by the English Language Liturgical Consultation. Used by permission. (8)

Thanksgiving 1: 'Holy and blessed are you, Lord our God'. Used by permission of the author, the Revd Dr J Charles Brock, Mansfield College, Oxford. (11)

Thanksgiving 3: 'We pray that you will make us', based on the French Reformed Church, Eucharistic Prayer II 1982, and published in *Baptism and Eucharist: Ecumenical Convergence in Celebration*, Max Thurian and Geoffrey Wainwright (eds.), 1983, WCC Publications, World Council of Churches, Geneva, Switzerland, pp. 153ff. (16/17)

Prayer after Communion: 'Accomplished and concluded', from the Liturgy of the Greek Orthodox Church. Used by permission of His Eminence the Archbishop of Thyateira and Great Britain. (19/20)

'You have opened to us the scriptures', from p. 40 of the *Book of Common Order*, 1979. © The Saint Andrew Press, Edinburgh. Used with permission. (20)

'Father of all we give you thanks', from *The Alternative Service Book 1980*. Copyright © The Central Board of Finance of the Church of England. (20)

SECOND ORDER OF WORSHIP

The English translation of the Nunc Dimittis, originally prepared by the International Consultation on English texts and revised in 1987 by the English Language Liturgical Consultation. Used by permission. (21, 29)

Prayer after Communion: 'Strengthen for service, Lord', Liturgy of Malabar. (29)

ACKNOWLEDGEMENTS

WEDDING SERVICE

'Gracious God, always faithful in your love for us', from p. 328 of the *Book of Worship: United Church of Christ*, published by the Office for Church Life and Leadership, St. Louis, Missouri. (51)

'Let your peace dwell', adapted from the Order of the Uniting Churches in Australia. (58)

'Blessed be God the Father.' Adapted from *The Alternative Service Book 1980* which is © The Central Board of Finance of the Church of England. (65)

FUNERAL SERVICE

'God, who gave us birth', from *The Funeral: A Service of Witness to the Resurrection, The Worship of God, Supplemental Liturgical Resource 4*. © 1986 The Westminster Press. Altered from *The Book of Services* and used by permission of The United Methodist Church, U.S.A. 1985. Used by permission of Westminster/John Knox Press.

'O God who brought us to birth', in Janet Morley, *All Desires Known*, Women in Theology and Movement for the Ordination of Women, 1988 (75); and 'Intimate God', in Janet Morley and Hannah Ward (eds.), *Celebrating Women*, Women in Theology and Movement for the Ordination of Women, 1986 (76). Both © Janet Morley. Used with permission.

Text of 'God of all consolation', from *The Rite of Funerals* © 1970, International Committee on English in the Liturgy, Inc. All rights reserved.

'Now that the earthly life', from the Order of the Uniting Churches in Australia. (79)

The English translation of the Te Deum originally prepared by the International Consultation on English texts and revised in 1987 by the English Language Liturgical Consultation. Used by permission. (79)

Alan Gaunt, 'As we give thanks for A . . ., we commit ourselves . . .'. Used by permission of the author. (81)

SERVICE FOR HEALING

'Almighty God to whom all hearts' from *The Alternative Service book 1980, adapted from The Book of Common Prayer (1662)*. The Alternative Service Book 1980 is © The Central Board of Finance of the Church of England. (4, 50, 107)

CREEDS AND CANTICLES

The English translation of the Lord's Prayer, Apostles' Creed and Nicene Creed, originally prepared by the International Consultation on English texts and revised in 1987 by the English Language Liturgical Consultation. Used by permission. (111, 113)